The Unfortunate Passion of Hermann Broch

José María Pérez Gay

Translated from the Spanish by Eduardo Jiménez Mayo

Floricanto Press

Original Title: *"Hermann Broch: Una pasión desdichada"*
from the collection of essays, *El imperio perdido*

ISBN 978-0-9796457-3-5

Floricanto Press
650 Castro Street, Suite 120-331
Mountain View, California 94041-2055
www.floricantopress.com

The Unfortunate Passion of Hermann Broch

Table of Contents

Preface

Having earned its author, José María Pérez Gay, the Austrian Cross for Arts and Sciences, this acclaimed, concise biography focuses on novelist Hermann Broch's preoccupation with his Austrian-Jewish heritage and examines his obsession with human mortality, social and moral decadence and mass psychology, specifically, in relation to the tragic historical events of the first half of the twentieth century.

In contrast to Franz Kafka's worldwide fame, the effect that Broch (and his colleague Robert Musil) had on the literary world outside Central Europe has remained, until quite recently, rather unappreciated. At the root of his profound literary achievement is his analytical clairvoyance concerning the crisis of values that would culminate in the ignominious catastrophes of the Second World War.

In his trilogy, *The Sleepwalkers*, praised by Milan Kundera as "one of the greatest European novels," Broch illustrates the decay of values in German society, combining lyricism, essayism and naturalism in three distinct segments, beginning with the demise of the Prussian aristocracy and shifting to the moral bankruptcy of the bourgeoisie. The nadir is reached in the third volume as a nihilistic Zeitgeist emerges, devoid of any moral or ethical principles. The depth of his political critique and his modernist experimentation with form and content undoubtedly owe much to the influence of James Joyce.

In *The Death of Virgil*, described by Thomas Mann as "one of the most extraordinary and profound experiments ever to have been undertaken with the flexible medium of the novel," Broch depicts the epic Roman poet's transformation of everything tangible into an inner, visionary, dream-like experience, as he faces the last hours of his life. The moribund poet, fatigued by the decadence of Roman civilization, carries on a discussion with Caesar Augustus, whereby the former, disenchanted with the efficacy of literature, calls for his work to be burned, while the latter wishes it to be preserved for posterity, for it captures the legacy of the Empire. A similar quest for the 'holy' within a world of eroding values becomes the subject of another of Broch's outstanding novels, *The Guiltless*.

In the midst of an era characterized by moral decadence, Hermann Broch wrestles with pessimism, though he clings to his belief in the capacity for human transcendence as the ultimate purpose of literary expression. Morally and spiritually speaking, he believes that literature must possess a restorative function. He also suggests that science alone is inadequate when faced with the task of grasping the world's totality. Moreover, he implies that perhaps the novelist is better equipped than the church and clergy to apprehend the metaphysical components of existence — for literature stands as the revelation of a mythic unity of being in the world, while men and women strive to come to terms with their mortality.

This book introduces us to the gentle, generous soul of one of Europe's greatest modern novelists, contributing to the recuperation of his legacy for the benefit of all those who embrace the moral dimensions of literature.

Susanne Kimball

The University of Texas at San Antonio

Author's Acknowledgements

The Unfortunate Passion of Hermann Broch constitutes the first of a series of essays I wrote based on a graduate seminar I taught from 1982-83, entitled, "Literature and Society in Austria (1880-1938)." The seminar was conducted in the Department of Sociology and Political Science at the National Autonomous University of Mexico (UNAM). Octavio Rodríguez Araujo, chairman of the department at the time, lent his full support to the course despite its unconventionality, and I am forever grateful to him for this. I am also greatly indebted to my students, whose feedback and participation contributed to the contents of this book, and among them I would like to give special recognition to the following: María del Carmen Gómez del Campo, Elisa Ramírez, Javier Nabia, Concepción Arroyo, Constanza Trujillo, Lidia Pico Herrera, Diego Cardona, Guadalupe Ordiales, Gina Zabludovsky, Alberto Saldívar and Carolina Lozoya.

It has been said that the task of writing a book may be likened to embarking on a voyage. Well, quite often the friends that come along with us for the ride represent the best part of the voyage. Those who came along with me on this voyage are the same ones who have always been there for me: Santa Alicia de las Mudanzas and my beloved Don Pepe, Héctor Aguilar Camín, Lilia Suárez, Abel Quezada, Luis Linares Zapata, José Joaquín Blanco, Ángeles Mastretta, Luis Miguel Aguilar, Fernando Solana Olivares, José Antonio Álvarez Lima, José Woldenberg, Rolando Cordera, Raúl Páramo Ortega, José Luis Martínez, Soledad Loaeza and Adrián Lajous Vargas.

I translated all the quotations in this series, without exception, directly from the German. Ultimately, my critique of the writers featured in this series and of their times was not intended to be other than personal in nature and intimate in scope.

Author's Introduction

Cultural Survival

The Austro-Hungarian Empire vanished at the beginning of the twentieth century, seemingly without a trace. This five-volume series is concerned with the fate of Austrian culture in the wake of the Austro-Hungarian Empire's demise. In it, the reader encounters a discussion of five exceptional Viennese writers — Hermann Broch (the present volume), Robert Musil (volume two), Karl Kraus (volume three), Joseph Roth (volume four) and Elias Canetti (volume five) — each one indispensable for understanding the aspirations, concerns, achievements and worldview of the Austrians at this crucial juncture in history. I have chosen to focus on these five authors because it is through their lives and work that one may gain a genuine appreciation of late Austro-Hungarian culture and the constructive and destructive impulses at work behind the scenes during the period of the Empire's ultimate demise, and on through to the advent of the Second World War. These writers did not take refuge in the past, nor did they concern themselves with dreams of a brave new world to come. Their works seem to be more concerned with subtleties of attitude rather than with ideas as such, and with nuances of character rather than universally applicable concepts.

For some time now, my readings of these five authors have confirmed me in my conviction that literature represents the most sanctifying dimension of life. Their poems, essays, aphorisms, novels, short stories, theater plays, chronicles, diaries and letters contribute to making the world a more habitable place. They refresh our spirits, help us catch our breath and restore our zest for life and love, endowing us with an improbable optimism. Literary criticism is not a career, as such, but a vocation that one awakens to while spending years of patient study dedicated to the assimilation of culture.

Vienna, at the dawn of the twentieth century, was the capital of a great empire. This city was the hub from which more than fifty million subjects were governed. Contained within the limits of the Empire were more than ten different ethnic groups speaking many different languages: Germans, Hungarians, Poles, Jews, Czechs, Slovaks, Croats, Serbs, Italians, Slovanians, Bulgarians, Romanians and Ruthians. The Hapsburgs, exercising four hundred years of hegemony, held dominion over numerous nations. Their subjects included eight million Germans, sixteen million Slavs, six million Italians, two million Jews, and two hundred thousand Gypsies. The Empire's northern frontier was Hilgesdorf, Bohemia (today's Czech Republic). Its southern frontier was Ostrawizzaberg, in present-day Yugoslavia. Its western limit was Rocca d'Angera on the banks of Lake Maggiore in present-day Italy. Its eastern limit was Chilischeny in Bukovina, integrated subsequently into the Soviet Union. The First World War was to erase the Austro-Hungarian Empire from the map. An entire European empire became extinct, and its distinctive culture would be largely annihilated during the period encompassing the First and Second World Wars (1914-1945).

One of the few legacies to survive the Empire's demise would be the works of Sigmund Freud. The founding father of psychoanalysis would continue to haunt us in the wake of his death, representing a world in which the reality of unconscious desires was manifest in the notorious Oedipus complex, a universe in which men were governed by the instinctual drives of life and death. Freud's writings cannot be divorced from his life, nor can his life be divorced from the history of the decline of Austria. His character was forged in the consensus and contradictions of that époque. The illusions, disenchantments, sufferings and expectations of his era are therefore apparent in his writings. His were achievements of the diagnostic sort, characterized by sober lucidity and laboriousness aimed at discovering the truth. His destiny was akin to that of

the Austro-Hungarian Empire in that his life would culminate in disenchantment — a process in which utopias are formed and deformed, and
one in which they collide and are shattered. After Freud, we no longer
imagine consciousness as a given, rather we see it as a construct.

However, in relation to the regeneration of Austrian culture, perhaps the figure that may claim even greater achievements than he is
the philosopher Ludwig Wittgenstein, an individual of exceptional intelligence, possessing one of the sharpest, richest and most profoundly
critical minds of the twentieth century. His writings were the result
of an intellectual passion and yearning for clarity so acute as to be un-
matched in the German tradition, except perhaps by Arthur Schopenhauer. Wittgenstein was an aeronautical engineer whose work, though
sustained for only a brief period, was solid and brilliant. He was also an
architect who built an exemplary home in the decade of the twenties.
Moreover, he was a sculptor of refined and admirable capabilities, an
extraordinary music director who may have reached the highest heights
in that field, a school teacher obsessed with the impartation of knowledge, a hermit who committed himself for months at a time to spiritual
and contemplative exercises, as well as a professor at Cambridge who
wrote and researched but never held class nor cared for academics. He
was an Austrian who held sway over British philosophy, and he was heir
to an enormous fortune that he distributed among various institutions
and friends.

Wittgenstein saw his conquest of the intellectual community in England as a reflection of the territorial conquests of the Austro-Hungarian
Empire: though, in a sense, both were ill fated. Years after his departure
from England, when professors at Oxford were studying and debat-
ing his work, Wittgenstein would affirm that that university was nothing but a territory in quarantine: an utterly sterile land, philosophically
speaking. Nevertheless, in the early forties analytical philosophy would
impose itself in England and the United States. The professors of the
Vienna Circle and Herbert Feigl at the University of Minnesota, Rudolf
Carnap at the University of Chicago, Eduard Zilsel, Felix Kaufmann,

mathematicians Kurt Gödel and Karl Menger, all turned their attention to questions of logic and the theory of knowledge and language. Their work abounds in scientific paradigms and it espouses the reclamation of a univocal clarity whereby rigorous justification is expected of each statement.

Eventually, a wide circle of students and intellectuals in foreign countries began to express curiosity in the origins of Austrian logical empiricism. Among these circles there was great interest in the pioneering work of Ernst Mach and Ludwig Boltzmann as well as great astonishment at the paintings of Gustav Klimt, Egon Schiele and Oskar Kokoschka. Furthermore, through the buildings of Richard Neutra — exiled in the United States — they were introduced to the architecture of Adolf Loos. They were introduced to Austrian jurisprudence through the teachings of Hans Kelsen at the University of California and they delighted in the music of Austrians Gustav Mahler, Anton Bruckner, Arnold Schönberg, Alban Berg and Anton Webern, the latter three being specialists in dodecaphonic compositions.

Another revelation for them was Joseph Schumpeter, a professor at Harvard University, who brought the Austrian brand of economics to the United States. He had been Minister of Finance under the First Austrian Republic and president of the Biedermann Bank of Vienna. He was a brilliant theoretician of economic cycles, an expert in the rhythms of industrial renovation and a forerunner in the diffusion of new technologies. Eugen Böhm-Bawerk's critiques of the concept of value-labor were also held in high esteem, while Rudolf Hilferding, Ludwig von Mises and Friedrich A. Hayek, theoreticians of neo-liberalism, were other favorites. The result was that by the end of the twentieth century, the Austrian brand of economics resurfaced with all its force and relevance, raising doubts and stimulating new propositions, prompting a reconsideration of some of the most vital problems — the system of international markets, the globalization of the economy and the critique of Marxist economic principles.

Freud, Wittgenstein and Schönberg continue to be consequential in our own times. While there are others whose influence may still be felt among us, the names of these three have taken a lofty place in the annals of world history. The literary legacy of the Austro-Hungarian Empire was equally substantial. The historical circumstances and agonies of the early twentieth century were transposed into poems, novels, short stories and other literary forms.

The Central European writers of this period [1880-1938] tended to draw us into a distinctive world, one in which happiness was not an option. Perhaps more than any of their contemporaries, Hermann Broch, Karl Kraus, Franz Kafka, Arthur Schnitzler, Joseph Roth, Robert Musil and Elias Canetti were able to express in their writings the sense of rupture and chronic anxiety at the heart of modernity. Moreover, in their work they paid homage to the power of the imagination. Despite their impressive accomplishments, the demise of the Empire meant that many of these writers would be temporarily forgotten, along with their efforts at forging a private, psychological and concrete representation of the relations between their own era and universal history. Rarely has there been such a graphic demonstration of the limits of culture in the face of barbarity as is evident in the lives of these men. By the close of the Second World War, there was hardly a remembrance of some of the aforementioned figures. In fact, in the fifties, the Nobel Prize Commission inquired in Austria about a novelist named Hermann Broch, and the Municipality of Vienna responded after a few weeks of investigation that no one in Vienna knew of a writer by that name.

It was George Steiner who observed that, with few exceptions, the greatest cultural achievements during the fall of the Austro-Hungarian Empire are attributable to the Jewish community. When one speaks of Freud, Wittgenstein, Kafka, Broch, Mahler or Schönberg, one is referencing one of the most glorious and simultaneously tragic chapters in the history of the Diaspora. It is a chapter that begins with the destruction of the Jewish ghettoes during the French Revolution, continues through the Imperial Napoleonic period, and culminates in the barbarity of the Third Reich. Vienna, the city of Kraus and Freud, was also the place where plans were first drawn up for the extermination of the Jewish race.

We are presently [the first Spanish edition of this book dates to 1991] witnessing an uncanny transformation of the societies of Central Europe. While socialist political and economic regimes have begun crumbling down one after another, the vestiges of Austro-Hungarian culture, the remains of her wrecked ship, have begun to resurface. States such as Hungary, Yugoslavia, Czechoslovakia, Poland and Romania are rediscovering the profound and problematic cultural diversity of their citizenry. Ethnic autonomy and ethnic conflict that the Soviet Union had attempted to suppress are gradually reasserting themselves. Behind the scenes of the political restructuring in the region lurks a boiling cauldron of ethnic strife, subversion and dissatisfaction. It appears that unresolved conflicts dating from the final century of the Austro-Hungarian Empire are the same ones that are currently returning to haunt and arrest the development of Central Europe.

The ongoing disintegration of the Soviet Union may be understood as harkening back to the earlier demise of the Austro-Hungarian Empire. Throughout the past seventy-three years [1917-1990], national tensions and conflicts have been destroying the country's precarious unity. The resistance of Lithuania, Estonia and Latvia and the rebellion of Moldavia and Georgia reveal a relentless struggle against centralized rule, suggesting that it may not be long before an alliance of independent states replaces the current system. The future of the Soviet Union, therefore, is inextricably linked to the destiny of the minority nations contained within it — those diverse, impetuous, rebellious, vigilant and haughty peoples who refuse to relinquish their national autonomy.

One of the most interesting aspects of the present crisis of socialism is the resurrection of the Austrian brand of Marxist theory, particularly those authors whom Stalinism condemned as traitors to the Marxist-Leninist tradition. Today, the world appears to be surprised at the revelation of nationalistic agendas in Central Europe, yet this is the very phenomenon that Otto Bauer, Karl Renner and Max Adler understood to be at the core of the crisis in the late Austro-Hungarian Empire. In fact, the solution that they posited to the problem of national minorities —

whom Friederich Engels defined as "ahistorical entities" — was one that embraced democratization. Austrian Social-Democrats recognized the importance of cultural diversity and the rights of minority nations and ethnic groups to self-determination. In their view, this premise would be the cornerstone for the construction of socialism and democracy in Central Europe.

The Austro-Hungarian Empire died as a political reality, however, the cultural legacy of the Empire has not vanished. Its heritage was kept alive in the cultural production of the exile community, as well as in the memory of their descendants, students and aficionados. The Empire's ghost continues to haunt the political evolution of Central Europe today, but undoubtedly, the greatest bequest we received from the late Austro-Hungarian Empire was its literary legacy, the abundant masterworks in fiction, reportage and other genres created by the five writers featured in this series. Literature was the preferred means of cultural survival for Hermann Broch, Robert Musil, Karl Kraus, Joseph Roth and Elias Canetti, and their writings continue to delight, engage and challenge us today. It is typically when we face the worst of times that the best of writers come to our rescue and their virtues shine with greater intensity than ever.

The Unfortunate Passion
of Hermann Broch

Where the Living Converse with the Dead

It was seven in the morning. Four young armed men were knocking at the door. They knocked several times to no response. Armbands with swastikas revealed their purpose. It was dawn. The cold March wind whistled as it passed through the crevices of the windows. Angela Sand, the housekeeper, had decided not to serve breakfast yet. The four militiamen entered and began asking questions about Hermann Broch.

The investigation, fortunately, was brief. The inhabitants of Altaussee, a town in the Austrian Alps, were well acquainted with the four National-Socialists, as well as with their relatives, homes and businesses; but with respect to Hermann Broch, they were at a loss. At first, no one seemed to know whom they were seeking. Finally, it was confirmed that there was indeed a Hermann Broch in town, that he was a Viennese professor who spent his winters in the home of the Geiringer family. It was about noon when they transferred him to the jail in Bad Aussee. The Viennese authorities were not responsible for ordering his arrest. As it happened, that morning — the thirteenth of March 1938 — the German army had occupied Austria. Unsuspectingly, Broch was one of the seventy thousand persons detained that month. Sixty thousand of them were Jews who were deported seven months later to the death camps of Auschwitz, Lublin, Minsk, Riga, Treblinka and Theresienstadt.

Nine or ten hours passed. His cell in Bad Aussee was very small, having two cots and a toilet. Around nine o'clock they fed him. He never could have imagined that the mailman of Alt Aussee, in order to demonstrate their strict vigilance of the local correspondence, had denounced him as a member of the Communist Party. Broch had been receiving weekly editions of the magazine *Das Wort*, which was produced in the Soviet Union. He immediately feared that his detention was a prelude to deportation, since he was a Jew and they might have discovered this fact. Why hadn't he emigrated two or three years before? His mother and son had impeded him from leaving. But another factor was his firm belief that England and France, and possibly Italy and Hungary, would oppose the annexation of Austria. He did his best to hide his fears of deportation, while he observed the presence of Austrian policemen dressed in German uniforms.

At dawn the following day, Angela Sand brought him his manuscripts and paper on which to write. That afternoon another detainee arrived, Joseph Khalss, leader of the Anti-Fascist Front of the local salt mines. Three days later, Gregor Angerer was incarcerated, a Social-Democrat militant. The cell was very narrow and one of the three had to sleep on the floor. That weekend, Broch couldn't get out of bed; he had no strength with which to do so. He had begun to suffer an intestinal hemorrhage. With each passing day he was paler, sadder and more indolent. Twice he was forced to traverse an ample patio to visit the interrogation room. It was one week after the invasion and it became clear that there would be no opposition. A feeling of fellowship arose between Broch and Khalss during their time in prison. They unhesitatingly confided in each other about their preoccupations.

For the next few days Broch appeared to be operating under a kind of imperative that obliged him to write. He began drafting, no less than ten times, the final chapter of his novel *The Death of Virgil*. He was convinced that his writing career was coming to a close and that he would be shipped at any moment to a concentration camp. He had trouble sleeping and anything that sounded like it might be the approaching Gestapo would cause him to jolt out of his cot.

The judge wasn't sure what to do with this detainee. Two weeks had passed and no one had been able to confirm the accusations against him. Bent on imparting justice, the judge turned him over to the region's chief political figure, Erich Dumann, who was of the opinion that Broch was an absentminded professor, a man with his head in the clouds, who knew nothing of mundane affairs. He managed to convince the Nazis of Altaussee that the suspect was harmless, making a point of his ill health, and he put him on a train bound for the capital.

On the fourth of April, Hermann Broch returned to Vienna. He was ordered to register at the Office for Political Investigations. The city had changed. Flags with the swastika hung from the principle edifices, decorating the Ringstrasse and the city center. That evening he witnessed one of those monstrous marches — solemn, somewhat funerary parades, carried out under beacon lights — of the kind that were celebrated continually in Germany under the Führer's egis. "Jail was almost paradise when compared to the collective psychosis I saw in the streets," wrote Broch. Broch didn't want to return to his family's home. The Gestapo was certainly staking it out. The persecution of the Jews caused him to land in Child Hospital with a severe case of ulcerous colitis. Upon his release, he took refuge in the home of Jadwigga Judd, a friend of his secretary Anna Herzog who had emigrated to France.

After two weeks, he finally returned to his apartment at Gonzagagasse. It was a fifteen-room condominium where the Broch family had lived for thirty years. As he reviewed his archives, he dedicated himself to finding a way out, yet he was not accustomed to political maneuvering. In these circumstances, and at fifty-two years old, what country would be willing to give him a visa? He had done the most ingenious, strange and contradictory things in the name of literature. In the name of literature he had auctioned his family's fabric and textiles factory eleven years prior, precisely when no one else was disposed to do so. In the name of literature he had taken refuge in a town in the Alps, when the ascent of fascism indicated that he should abandon Austria. And in the name of literature, although recognizing his error and confessing it, he was now headed down a dead end street. He had been cast in the role of a fugitive, yet a single certainty drove him on — literature is, as José Emilio Pacheco once said, the only clarification of our burdensome human experience and the only place where the living communicate with the dead.

In the month of April, he took to traveling at night on the urban trains, with no particular direction, getting on and getting off at different stations, until he was sure that no one was following him. In those days, partisans of National-Socialism were taking news to the Gestapo regarding the details of the complots being hatched in Vienna. Attentive to all suspicious activities, these informers worked in the shadows. Their victims were the Jews. The Austro-Fascists were the incarnation of meanness, the uncontainable rancor of the petty bourgeoisie, dominant and ferocious, pitted against the fear and meekness of the Jewish community. In that ambience of anti-Semitism, there was a palpable and almost definite sense of doom. Gossip was circulating profusely regarding future mass deportations. These forebodings would soon materialize with the furious exterminations that would cost the lives of millions of people. For the Nazis, the Austrian *Anschluss* represented a step toward the union of the sanitary forces of Arian Europe in a combined effort against worldwide Judaism. Hitler fomented hatred toward Austria-Hungary from the start. In that lost empire was encoded the effigy of the enemy: its abstract unity, the artificial union of states and nations that differed in language and blood, became an object of Hitler's ridicule. He loathed its universal eclecticism, its parliamentary system and carefree libertinage, which, according to him, were the decadent bi-products of democracy. In his eyes, Austria-Hungary was a Babylonian kingdom, a garrulous institution marked by the deceitful political maneuverings of the Jews.

Hermann Broch scheduled an appointment with the newspaperman Louis Barcata in the Café Promenaden. Prior to the German occupation, that is where journalists met from the newspaper *Die neue freie Presse*. Now this place was frequented by editors paralyzed by fear, lack of enthusiasm or the disintegration of their faith; and many journalists were infected with the pessimism that held the impossibility of Nazi defeat or the liberation of Austria. After a long wait, Louis Barcata arrived, a young reporter that had written an article about Broch on the occasion of his fiftieth birthday. As a precautionary measure, should the Gestapo detain him and destroy his originals, he conferred on Barcata the first draft his novel, *Bewitchment*. The wife of Barcata was traveling to Stockholm and from Sweden she would send the manuscript to Willia and Edwin Muir, Broch's translators in England.

"There's not much I can do," said Broch. "Sooner or later someone will denounce me. There are two locksmiths living at Gonzagagasse. I employed one of them a few years back. Fearing that the other would denounce me, I invited him to my home and invented all sorts of repairs for him to perform. Yesterday he thanked me that I, a pure Arian, should show consideration for an old Jewish locksmith who had fallen on hard times."

The First Automobiles

Jews were being detained and beaten in the streets. Those who couldn't demonstrate proof of their imminent departure from Austria were deported to a concentration camp, or they were jailed until relatives or friends presented a consulate visa or paid an emigration tax. "The most repugnant thing about these political measures," wrote Broch, "was that they were done for money, because behind it all was the desire to appropriate the Jewish fortunes. I, for my part, did all I could to salvage a fraction of our family's capital and ensure my mother's financial situation."

A month later, in May of 1938, the Gestapo organized the first of the pogroms in Vienna. They detained some six hundred Jews and deported them immediately to Dachau, a death camp dear Munich. Broch feared for his life then and for his mother's life. The old woman lived in their apartment at Gonzagagasse and she refused to leave Vienna. "Nothing will be done to the elderly," she used to say. After the first pogrom, Hermann Broch understood that barbarity had been unleashed and was roaming free. Jews kept away from any public gatherings as if they had the plague. They were prohibited from entering the parks, nor could they visit theaters, cinemas or museums, and their children were expelled from school. Broch decided to negotiate with his ex brother-in-law, Rudolf, the transference of his mother to Cseperg, Hungary, to the residence of the Von Rotermann family. But Johanna Broch feared them more than the Nazis. She did accept, however, a second proposal, and she moved to the apartment of Ea von Allesch, ex-wife of her son, since she offered the security of being Arian. Toward the end of May,

Broch sold the last rooms of his apartment at Gonzagagasse. He helped his mother prepare for her move and he returned to the apartment of Jadwigga Judd. The other members of the family weren't in danger. At twenty-eight, Hermann Broch von Rotermann, his son, was an aristocratic Catholic residing in Athens, and his brother Fritz always was a man of good fortune. Fritz had accumulated capital in gold, made investments and emigrated to Cambridge, Massachusetts, where he exercised the profession of engineering.

For two months Hermann Broch searched for a visa in the consulates of England, France, Denmark, Switzerland and the United States. All his efforts seemed useless. Despite having sold his parents' fabric and textile factories, he didn't have enough money to guarantee his residence in a foreign country. Reality had been conspiring against him. One morning he wanted to revalidate his passport, but the Ministry of Foreign Affairs retained it without explanation.

While his negotiations were floundering in Vienna, Broch's secretary, Anna Herzog, sought out a man in Paris named Paul Schrecker, a good friend of the writer, who suggested that he contact James Joyce. The next morning, Anna went to James' domicile, 7 Rue Edmond Valentin, with the idea of leaving a message. Nora Joyce opened the door in her pajamas. "Are you a journalist?" she shouted at Anna Herzog. "No, I'm here on behalf of the Austrian writer…" "Are you a journalist?" interrupted Joyce himself. "Tell me what newspaper has sent you here!" "Hermann Broch," Anna stammered, "needs help."

After a lengthy explanation, Anna implored his assistance. James Joyce had never met him, though both had the same editor, Daniel Brody, owner of the publishing house Rhein Verlag. Joyce had read his novel *The Sleepwalkers*, and, more importantly, his essay "James Joyce and the Present." It affirmed that Joyce had brought to the English language the sentiments of foreign languages, adding that his vast knowledge of French and German literature was not in vain. If it hadn't been for Joyce's experimentations in theme, Broch argued, contemporary literature would not have experienced such a profound renewal: "*Ulysses* rides about like a mythical horseman through the obscurity of time and of all eternity. We don't know where James's road will lead us. Therein lie the dangers of an ascending deviation, the consequence of his pessimism along with the force of his literary ability placed at the service of his own despair. On the other hand, the more Joyce approaches a sense of totality, an objective of which he himself is skeptical, the denser and more complicated become the scheme of symbols and associations in whose labyrinth life transpires. The more intense the obligation of producing a universal work, the more threatening the danger of the infinite, and the infinite and death are children of one and the same mother." Joyce was fascinated with the essay. He felt that it was one of the few intelligent critiques of his work and he appreciated its adverseness to hollow solemnity. In effect, the essays of Hermann Broch, pillar of his literature, never were dogmatic or cynical sketches. They typically avoided the illusory straight line as a means of proceeding from one point to another. His essays were rather like a compass, oscillating between discovery and amazement.

Joyce acceded to getting him a visa. His friend, Benjamin Creémieux, pointed out that he was the right man for the job. A week later he telephoned Anna Herzog and announced that the French consulate in Vienna had already received the order to grant him a visa. But despite the intervention of Creémieux, three weeks passed without results. Hermann Broch went there every morning. He waited hours, and upon arriving at the window he was informed that there was no visa there in his name. Procuring the visa became an obsession for Joyce. He called Anna Herzog some ten or fifteen times a day. There was no explanation for what had gone wrong. Creémieux assured him that the visa was waiting in Vienna. This was in fact the case. The problem was that the French consul couldn't deliver the visa to Broch because he was without his passport. Yet, for its own part, the Ministry of Foreign Services demanded the visa in order to return his passport to him. Otto Kiebacher, Broch's lawyer, broke this vicious cycle with an astute argument, but it came too late. Eduard Daladier, the new French Prime Minister, had prohibited the entrance of more Austrian immigrants and the consulate was obliged to cancel his visa.

Two weeks later, Edwin Muir initiated the negotiations to obtain a visa from the British government. James Joyce made it clear that he could do nothing in this case. "I am Irish. I am not and will never be English," he told Anna Herzog. "I don't want to and can't do anything for him in England. In any case, let me see if Stephen Hudson can arrange something, though I don't believe it is possible."

After various interviews with his friends at the Foreign Office, Hudson obtained the visa. But the comedy of equivocations continued. The British consulate had mistakenly remitted the document to Anna Herzog's residence in Paris. On June 20, 1938, Hermann Broch finally received the visa. It was a permit of residence in England for three months. Meanwhile, the American consulate in Vienna notified him that Albert Einstein and Thomas Mann had written letters on his behalf, and that his solicitation of residence in the United States would be reviewed. Broch couldn't wait any longer. Upon leaving the British Legation he headed for the offices of KLM and purchased an airplane ticket to London via Rotterdam.

The morning of July 29, 1938, Hermann Broch boarded a taxi bound for Asperm Airfield. During the drive he saw the avenues and forests of Vienna for the last time. How could one describe the transformation of spirit and lifestyle of those who had lived in Vienna, now under Nazi occupation, during the past fifty years? The inhabitants of Hungarian, Czech, Polish or Italian origin of the Old Empire had remained Austrians, but not Austrians of the age of splendor, rather of one which was marked by a period of ultimate decadence. The inhabitants of Vienna remained culturally German in their majority, not as members of a great civilization, rather as the rubble of a depopulated world. Broch had inhabited the city for fifty years, bearing witness to the Empire's twilight, and now, under Nazi occupation, the city appeared to him as a wasteland. It is understandable, therefore, that he should wish to invoke the years of his childhood, the more pleasant atmosphere of his summer holidays at the Villa of Purkesdorf with its large, perpetually open windows through which the wind and the scent of chestnut trees could be perceived, and those unforgettable afternoons in turn-of-the-century Vienna in which he had discovered with astonishment the first automobiles passing along the Ringstrasse.

The Expiation of His Past

Broch believed that the writer's vocation has its roots in his early infancy, yet he revealed very little about his childhood. The letters that do narrate a few scenes of his early years date to the 1940s. And he never kept a diary. "In my incorrigible laziness, I never wrote a page in a diary [...] If I had written an autobiography, I would have failed, due to lack of material." His essay "Autobiography as a Program of Work" (1941) demonstrates a suspicious indifference toward self-revelation. "The text is autobiographical only because it deals with issues that are coincidentally contemporary to my own life [...] In any case, I share this with Kafka and Musil. None of us really have a biography. We have lived and written; that is all." Nonetheless, six months before his death, Hermann Broch wrote: "An irrational structure sustains the occupation of the writer, one which is formed before he turns six years old. What happens later is no longer irrational or literary. It is presented to us then in the forms of precise recollections and rational strategies. The literary quality is linked to that irrational part, however. When I write something worthwhile, I realize that it comes from the first years of my childhood."

If the European aristocrat had a legendary familial history, the Jewish bourgeois had only the history of his neurosis: "You come from a very neurotic family," writes Broch to his son in 1949. "Your grandfather was a manic depressive with gleams of brilliance, your grandmother an obsessive neurotic of the first order. A woman of little intelligence, vain, domineering and unreasonable." An inferno came to reside among the Austrian-Jewish families of the turn of the century, and it was preserved and even fortified thanks to their pathology. The decadent social climate signified the ruin of its traditional cultural attributes — work, sweat and austerity.

At seventy, Hermann Broch was still expiating his past: "While my mother protected my brother, I remained outside of her consideration and affection. My brother won the battle. That's why at age three I wanted to castrate my father and obliterate my brother [...] When I was a child, this jealousy very nearly consumed me. Fantasies of suicide haunted my childhood [...] I've been running from them ever since."

Paul Michael Lützeler has reconstructed the life of the writer as no one before him in his book, *Hermann Broch, Eine Biographie* (1986). He recognizes that the function of this literary genre, as with many others, is to capture in an effective synthesis all the cultural processes of a given society. But at the same time he knows, as Isaac Bashevis Singer once said, that the true life of a person can never be written because it is beyond the power of literature: "A complete life of any person would turn out to be as boring as incredible." Lützeler has dedicated many years not just to the biography of Broch, but also to the critical edition of his complete works. To him we owe a wise perspective on the work of this author, as well as the knowledge of many of the major events in his life.

Toward the end of the eighteenth century the Broch family abandoned the Ukraine and emigrated to Bohemia. Joseph Broch, the father, born February 12, 1851, was the youngest of twelve siblings. His grandfather was a sort of miracle-worker rabbi, specialist in the Talmud and an exceptional mathematician. At age twelve, Joseph fled his home and took refuge in Vienna, working in a textile shop. By the time he was twenty-five he was already known as one of the most gifted merchants in the city — a hard and brazen man, fond of taking risks, with an infallible nose for business and passionate about the future of the textile industry. In this sense, Broch shared something with Kafka and also with Hugo von Hofmannsthal. Hermann Kafka, the father of Franz, had overcome poverty in Prague; the grandfather of Hofmannsthal, Issac Löw, had achieved a title of nobility through his success in the textile industry and his great fortune. Joseph Broch started off working as an errand boy in the warehouses. Years later he would become the largest exporter of textiles in the entire Empire. No one described his ascension as well as Hermann Broch himself in his essay, "Hofmannsthal and His Time" (1948): "As a result of the edict that the emperor pronounced toward the end of the eighteenth century, an increased immigration of Jewish merchants occurred, particularly of those originating from the ghettoes of Moravia and Bohemia, and most chose to settle in Vienna. Even after the edict's annulment no one could divert, much less turn back, the tidal wave of emigrants. They had abandoned the provincial life believing that now they would once again be able to carry their precious culture from one country to another, as was the case in their former migrations. They never suspected that this time everything would be different. They were met with intolerance and it was demanded that they assimilate to the culture of the Hapsburg Empire. The magnetism of the metropolis, especially one like Vienna where capitalism flourished, centered around the allure of money."

Many of these Jews acquired an exemplary wisdom in their dealings with the majority population. "They learned to adjust to the needs of Viennese consumers and they also learned to deal in cattle, grains and textiles. They knew that by establishing themselves in Vienna they were presented with a chance at earning great profits. The country was at war and the army was their principal client." Joseph Broch navigated his way through that river of immigrants and surmounted all the obstacles. In the decade of the nineties, he acquired a factory of fabrics and textiles in Teesdorf — a town near Vienna — and he transformed it into one of the most productive in the Austro-Hungarian Empire. Kafka's father assured himself of prestige by arranging marriage with the daughter of a Jewish patrician, while Joseph Broch contracted matrimony with Johanna Schnabel, the eldest daughter of one of the best-situated families in Vienna, whose history dated back to the sixteenth century.

Hermann Broch was born in Vienna, November 1, 1886. His infancy was marked by his mother's rebuff of him and her favoritism toward his brother Fritz, though it is uncertain to what degree we may consider his viewpoints to be objective. His parents' marriage was a failure that he wouldn't understand until he reached maturity. His father, it turns out, was a homosexual. His children utterly feared him as they would fear a night bogey. And as if on principle, he enjoyed punishing them frequently. "Above all things," said my father, "a child should be punished. I was left-handed and they rid me of it with beatings." When the adolescent Hermann Broch decided to give himself wholly to industry and commerce, he was obeying paternal orders, for sure, but above all he was searching in that activity for the security that he required. In those days wealthy Jews tended to send their children to liberal arts high schools and colleges, though they were equally supportive if they chose a career in the sciences or if they wanted to dedicate themselves to painting or music. Excluded from titles of nobility, the Jews pursued notoriety by triumphing in the sciences and the arts. This enlightened attitude of the bourgeois Jews facilitated the flourishing of the sciences, the fine arts and music in Vienna at the dawn of the twentieth century.

But Joseph Broch did not interest himself in scientific or cultural prestige. He prohibited his son Hermann from enrolling in the high school for the humanities and years later he would do the same with respect to his university education. Broch passed the years of his infancy and adolescence in public schools. He wasn't happy there, but neither was he particularly unhappy. The intransigence of his father, always disposed to demonstrate to his children the absolute value of money, remained indestructible. The two brothers were raised together as enemies — never did a fraternal sentiment unite them, neither were they united in mutual dreams or aspirations. Thirty years later, when both were exiled in the United States, they hardly visited each other. "My relationship with Fritz is neutral. Every once and awhile I tell him the bitter truth; I make him see his meanness," Broch wrote, "such as his voracity for the paternal inheritance; and he swallows it all without a word." A decisive period in Broch's life was the one that commenced with his discovery of his father's homosexuality and ended with his decision to study textile engineering. In 1907 he took his degree in the College of

Fabrics and Textiles of Mühlhausen, in the French province of Alsace. Broch must have studied intensively, since he invented a machine for mixing diverse textiles which, in collaboration with the director of the College, he patented in Vienna in 1908.

"All in the name of cotton," was his lemma. Hermann Broch traveled to the United States in September of 1907. He visited New York, Chicago, Atlanta and New Orleans. He stayed for a week in Memphis, enabling him to buy cotton and participate in the "International Cotton Buyers and Spinners Conference" that was celebrated in nearby Atlanta. Upon returning to New York he visited Niagara Falls and was housed in the home of the Wolf family, friends of his father and owners of various factories of textiles and fabrics in Bohemia. Broch began to demonstrate a certain financial astuteness, as evidenced by his undeniable success in negotiating with industrialists in America where he had made contacts and took the utmost advantage of the doors that had been opened to him. His father's severity subsided somewhat in those years. The young industrialist enjoyed the approval of a father who was satisfied with his son's studies and his entrepreneurial success. But conflict between father and son would arise once more in 1907. On returning to the United States Broch met on a train one Franziska von Rotermann: a blue-eyed blond-haired young lady, daughter of Rudolf and Maria von Rotermann, sugar merchants from Hungary and members of the national aristocracy. Franziska's grandfather, an engineer from Hamburg, had emigrated to Budapest in 1860 and had offered his services in one of the factories of the Esterházy family, authentic feudal barons and proprietors of more than two hundred and ninety thousand hectares of fertile soil in the heart of Central Europe. Twenty years later her father received the title of *Ritter* (knight) von Rotermann for his services to the Hungarian economy. In time the Rotermanns became one more family in the national aristocracy. They forgot their German past and appropriated the local manners and customs. They also adopted the Hungarian nobility's rancor and disgust toward the Hapsburgs, who never included them in their state councils and always kept them at a distance. The Rotermanns lived as the Magyar landowners lived. They devoted themselves to hunting, kept stables with thoroughbred horses, organized parties of three days in the countryside, and spent the winter in Italy, among the groves of their Roman or Florentine gardens, with all their pomp, amenities and melancholies.

In the beginning, the Von Rotermann family opposed Franziska's marriage to Hermann Broch. The anti-Semitism of the Hungarian gentry and their disgust for upstart industrialists made all negotiations impossible. Joseph Broch would not allow discussion on the matter of a Christian wedding. He never accepted Franziska and he didn't consider her to be his son's fiancée. At the start of the summer of 1908, Rudolf von Rotermann wanted to separate his sister from the Viennese engineer, and to that end he proposed a long vacation on the Côte d'Azur, but his initiative failed because Broch followed Franziska there. When they returned from France they spent some days alone in Vienna. The Ringstrasse then was an autumn garden offering an ambience of attenuated melancholy to those indecisive lovers. Weeks later, on the patios of the Hirmer Villa — the Rotermann's residence Folszerfalva — Hermann Broch and Franziska were married. For over one year Broch frequented the Hermer Villa. On weekends he would ride horses with Franksiska's brothers. He also fenced with ability and passion, and on Sundays they united to write a collective novel, *Sonia*, the final chapter of which Broch penned with his brother-in-law.

The young engineer with his angular face, deep-set eyes and dark hair, was something of a dandy, and he measured six feet two inches tall. He possessed an alert gaze, a warm voice and a sober elegance. A sophisticated observer would recognize that his suits had been cut to measure by Samuel Ebstein, the best tailor in Vienna — grays and dark blues in winter, white and beige linens in July and August, shirts of white silk, black ties of woven wool, and Coyle or Early shoes. His summer trips to and weeklong stays in the Hirmer Villa were ever more frequent. Broch's sensibility and discretion completely seduced the Rotermann.

His indubitable affinities with that family led to his conversion to Roman Catholicism in 1909. In autumn he assumed the post of sub-director of the Vienna factory and in December he married Franziska, against the will of his parents. From the start, conjugal life was an irritating struggle for both of them. Franziska's dowry, a considerable amount for the time, pacified the wrath of Joseph Broch. The capital was invested in his factory. Despite his post as sub-director Broch did not earn a good salary, but his wife insisted on living with the luxuries to which she was accustomed. The controversy with his father was painful for Broch. Franziska gradually took on a secondary role in his life, though they had a baby boy together. They lived between Vienna and Teesdorf. They frequented Vienna's high society and the factory was in full expansion. Franziska, time and again, would interfere with his ability to manage the factory, and she ultimately became something of an enemy to him.

They had nothing in common, they discovered, except a score of disagreements, complaints and rancor. Broch managed temporarily to avoid Franziska's aggressiveness, while remaining distant from her parents, yet the inevitability and urgency of their separation was becoming apparent. Broch worked himself to exhaustion. He began to live a solitary life and he even began to consider a change of profession. It seemed to him that he would be better suited to the study of philosophy.

An Eternal Penitence

The ten years following their marriage belonged to a decade of turmoil. On September 2, 1908, Emperor Franz Joseph celebrated the seventieth year of his reign. By November of 1918, all this was but a memory. His armies were decimated and the Austro-Hungarian Empire had been erased from the face of the map. The night of September 2, however, he made an appearance at a gala function in the Hofoper Theater. The countess Christiane Thun-Slom had written *The Dream of the Emperor*, an opera in one act, during which some three hundred actors of the Burgtheater and the Staatsoper sang and danced "Aus der Heimat" ("From Our Fatherland"). Songs and dances of the thirteen nations of the Empire paraded across the stage. The final scene employed an allegorical concept: The many nations were united as one under their Emperor. That gala function was one of his first public reappearances. After the death by firing squad of his brother in Mexico, the suicide of his son and murder of his wife, Franz Joseph died of sadness in his palace.

On that evening, designed to pay homage to the Emperor, the Hofoper Theater gathered together in one stroke practically the entire high-class society of the Austro-Hungarian Empire. The Rotermann occupied the seventh box seat from the left. Franziska showed off a brocaded ivory silk dress; and next to her, Hermann Broch wore a tailcoat especially made for the occasion. On the first floor were the archdukes and the great dukes and duchesses of the House of Hapsburg. The Emperor arrived in a field marshal's uniform accompanied by the duchess Maria Theresa von Württemberg and her daughter, the princess Gisela von Bayern.

Upon leaving the Hofoper Theater that night, none of the invited took notice of a young painter who observed them as they departed in their carriages. What that young man really wanted was to "become somebody" in the world of art, to become an artist. He exercised in Vienna the errant bohemian lifestyle, lingering in cafés and bars full of losers. His works consisted of copies of postcards which he sold in the cantinas. His reproductions were of so little interest that even the stodgy Academy of Fine Arts rejected Adolf Hitler.

The politics of Franz Joseph and his administration, quite in line with the more conservative ideologies of the nineteenth century, possessed a certain similarity to the so-called democratic structures of Ancient Greece — i.e. liberty and equality for a few patricians perched atop the back of the great masses of plebeians. The Upper House in parliament was the direct expression of archaic powers. The Reichsrat (Austrian parliament) remained in the hands of the princes of the royal family, of archbishops and other Catholic prelates, of the heads of the great land-owning families, of the nobles whose seats were hereditary, and of other notables with lifelong appointments. The Upper House of the Hungarian parliament (Forendihaz) was an assembly of wealthy aristocrats, dignitaries of the Catholic and Orthodox Churches, and businessmen. The Emperor conferred titles of nobility on magnates, medical doctors, and university professors, who in reality were nothing but spokesmen for the landowning aristocracy. Parliament fought tooth and nail to maintain the submission of the national minorities and to preserve the unity of the Empire. Despite its efforts, in less than ten years, Austria-Hungary was whipped by turbulent waves of rancor and disconcertedness. The unity of the thirteen nations was but an illusion conjured up that night on the stage of the Hofoper Theater.

During the First World War Hermann Broch excused himself from military service to his superior at the Teesdorf factory of fabrics and textiles for reasons of ill health. He was traveling to the city of Vienna where he would be negotiating with contractors and bargaining with the chamber of commerce and the municipal authorities. The Great War was prolonged more than what the Austrian military officials had imagined, and the specter of defeat began to loom over them. Broch decided to set up a hospital in Teesdorf, procuring a supply of medicines and equipment. He housed military doctors in his home and it was under these circumstances that he learned of the horrors of the trenches. Though he had accomplished increasing productivity, a rapture of patriotism on the part of Joseph Broch practically led to the bankruptcy of their enterprises. Joseph decided to transfer his deposits from Switzerland — half of all his capital — to a Vienna bank, in order to invest them in the last series of war bonds, thereby helping to finance the Austro-Hungarian army. A stroke of good luck prevented disaster. Hermann informed his superior one morning that enormous quantities of cotton shipped by his father to neutral ports before the war were at the disposition of the company at the same low prices of 1913. In the early twenties the Broch firm had acquired two new factories and invested money in machines. It was then that his father retired. The lack of accord with his children was permanent. His two sons, in his eyes, were irresponsible and useless. There was some truth in this. After his separation from Franziska, Hermann wanted to sell the business and bury himself in his books; for his part, Fritz was in the habit of chasing after the first attractive woman that crossed his path. In his old age Joseph Broch fell like an old tree. He decided to erase his past and shed his memory. It seems that forgetfulness was a remedy against his chronic ill humor. Amnesia was the repairing void that compensated for his obsession with eternal penance. Joseph Broch became an eccentric in Viennese society. He was transported in a carriage pulled by two white horses and driven by a lackey suited in a livery uniform. Every morning at eleven he passed along the Ringstrasse, stopping off at the Panopticum, and for a time he attended the movies regularly in the afternoons.

His son Hermann, once a captain of industry, was now nursing a fanatical literary vocation. He read the works of Kant, Schopenhauer and Weininger and wrote some notes for an aesthetic system, as well as pieces on physics and mathematics. But he lacked clarity of direction. "I like science and investigation," he noted, "perhaps my true talent is to be found there." *Cantos 1913*, his first literary text, stands as an example of vocational irony. Moreover, in this text one can already notice the theme that was to dominate his future works — the degradation of values, a central concern in his novels *The Sleepwalkers* and *The Guiltless*. Equally significant are his contemporaneous essays on kitsch and the genealogy of its maximum exemplars: Nero, William II and Adolf Hitler.

Many of Broch's earliest essays, especially the first ones dedicated to Adolf Loos, were critical of the new currents of art and painting such as naturalism and impressionism, and the "Art-pour-l'art" movement, as well as of the works of composers such as Richard Wagner, Gustav Mahler and Richard Strauss. At that time Broch only favored two artists: Van Gogh and Oskar Kokoschka. In 1911 he wrote: "Ornament: The Loos Case," a pamphlet that he filed away in his drawers and never published. Though he was truly one of the great renovators of Austrian architecture, Broch refers to Loos disparagingly as "the apostle of utility" (Zweckmässigkeit). Regarding the scandal that Loos' building in Vienna's Michaelerplatz caused ("a nude and unornamented" building constructed outside the Imperial Palace), Broch wrote: "The old art is at the point of disappearing, and we are all in agreement on that. But anyone who despises ornament as much as Adolf Loos, as evidenced in his book *Ornament and Crime*, refuses to understand that ornament is the essence of art, the culmination of the artistic spirit. I maintain that Loos' own words could be used against him: 'Architects are merely bricklayers who speak Latin.'" One should note that Broch wrote this essay when he was twenty-four years old, and twenty-three years later, in 1933, he would publish *Cosmogony of the Novel*, where he sustained an opinion on art and ornament that was quite distinct, if not entirely opposed, to his earlier views. In short, the Broch of his forty-seventh birthday and beyond had definitively changed his views regarding ornament in art, and it appears that he never wrote about Loos again.

Between 1910 and 1914, Broch and many Austrians of his generation fell under the spell of the satirical journalist Karl Kraus. Kraus' enemies were shamed by his articles in *Die Fackel*, combustible for enflaming those spirits adverse to the war and the social ills of the time. Reading Kraus, Broch familiarized himself with the both the radiance and the shadows of everyday life. While the Great War devoured Europe, Broch worked in his factory; and at night he was a constant writer, proud of his solitary production.

He attended university and studied the sciences, transiting through mathematics and physics, dedicating himself to comprehending the work of Rudolf Carnap and the precepts of Axiomatic Geometry. Broch even sketched his own ideas on a system regarding the basic functions of logic, a condensed synthesis of logic and mathematics. Conversely, his study of philosophy led him to profound disappointments: "I realized that I couldn't even ask a single question about metaphysical issues. I was full of questions and nobody could give me answers." Around that time the natural sciences had arrived at a high point in their history, while philosophy sought to imitate their precision and exactitude. The result was a certain relativism whereby "truth and morality assumed a mere pragmatic function such that when young people wanted to ask advice of philosophy she declared herself incapable of giving it." The critique of positivism which Broch articulated energetically in his text, *The Spirit in an Unspiritual Age* (1934), dates to those times.

In 1912 he had written: "Positivism is at heart an enemy of philosophical reflection. All the problems that cannot be treated rationally are expelled to the realm of mysticism and the irrational. The positivists claim that 'authentic' philosophy cannot acquire knowledge of this realm. From its inception, philosophy has sought the rational comprehension of the totality of the world [...] but the positivist agenda dissolved the cosmogony of the universe (*Weltbild*), shattering its unity." He found himself in opposition to the positivistic trends of the time: delivering himself to investigations, doubts and values that the theorists of Austrian positivism didn't share with him. Ultimately, Broch opted for literature: "Nobody can destroy our metaphysical necessities; if that were possible all reflection would disappear [...] Even positivist philosophy would be impossible under such circumstances. If the religious exit is no longer viable then we should satisfy these necessities where they persist in indestructible form: in the individual. Literature has always been the outlet for these preoccupations [...] Literature represents a constant thirst for knowledge, an absolutely legitimate thirst."

Max Weber defined modern culture as the process toward the independence and autonomy of values. This process is coincidental to the birth of science, morality and modern art. In modernity we witness the disintegration of the *substantial ratio* incarnate in religion and metaphysics. The relativism that Broch criticized as a result of the hegemony of science was none other than the process of Western secularization. Since then, all problems that have to do with truth, justice and taste can be treated in terms of their own unique logic. For Broch, the autonomy of values represented a state of anarchy — the dynamics of Western modernity not only led to the loss of God but also to the ruination of Platonic cosmogony. Modernity would inevitably destroy the "absolute," archetypical and non-earthly values which had rendered existence meaningful in antiquity.

In the summer of 1918, Max Weber gave a series of lectures at the University of Vienna. In one of them he returned to the theme he was most passionate about: the diagnosis of his era. Weber saw the sign of his times in the return of a new polytheism; the ancient struggle of the gods had assumed the form of an irreconcilable antagonism between diverse orders of values. The modern world was devoid of sense because distinct value systems were conflicting in a fight to the death. Regarding these gods and their struggles, said Weber, science holds no sway for it is destiny that prevails. It was not due to bitterness or discontent that he would criticize those who envisioned redemption in science and who pretended to identify science and socialist revolution with the inexorable march of progress. Instead there was an admirable audacity in his signaling that the modern world had rendered existence senseless. The unity that could no longer be established in the social order needed to be sought after in the intimate life of the individual. Despite the catastrophes of his personal biography, he would learn to take courage in the midst of desperation: for in his despondency he would discover the seeds of hope.

Weber and Broch held identical positions with respect to the history and intellect of modernity, and their vocation for recognizing the limits and dangers inherent in it were akin. They were both engaged in the same struggle against the illusions of modernity with the intention of rescuing the individual from dissolution. However, in sharp contrast to Max Weber, Broch affirmed the existence of an absolute and transcendent ethical value that would confer on human life a dimension of exceptionality. Such an ethical ideal of culture implies the resurrection of an order centered on the certainty that life is in and of itself the supreme good, the supreme value, one in which death signifies the total absence of value. This conviction, present in all the works and attitudes of Hermann Broch, is quite similar to that of Christianity. The doctrine of Jesus of Nazareth, announced in the midst of the agony of the Roman Empire, is founded on the belief in his victory over death. The anguish of the demise of a worldly empire is compensated for by the faith in another, heavenly and everlasting. The end of the world is near but we will survive. We are by definition mortal, yet the forces of destruction will not prevail over us. In his novel, *The Sleepwalkers*, Broch included various chapters on the decline of values in which he affirms that the destruction of the Catholic cosmogony was a homicidal act of the rationalization processes of the West. Modernity sacrificed our lives and our priorities to a world condemned to extinction. His perspective on modern times presupposes the affirmation of eternal life as well as the condemnation of death (*summum malum*) as the incarnation of evil.

European intellectuals of the First World War lent a philosophical dignity to death that it had never enjoyed before, except perhaps in the political theory of Thomas Hobbs. They were a monomaniacal generation bent on execrating all culture and replacing liberalism with the nihilist theories of Nietzsche. Theirs was a generation that would witness the destruction of countless illusions and the abolition of numerous utopias, the horror of Verdún and the failure of Versailles, and the corruption of democracies bent on oppressing weaker nations. It was a generation that would bear witness to the many obstacles facing the liberation of subservient countries, to a series of inconclusive revolutions and to the ultimate dissolution of the Austro-Hungarian Empire.

The First Weak Man

On November 3, 1918, Italy and Austria signed an armistice and the Great War came to an end. The Austro-Hungarian Empire was divided in six national states, among them, three of Slavic origin: Yugoslavia, Czechoslovakia and Poland. Then, what was bound to happen, happened: On November 12, Karl Seitz, the Social-Democrat leader, proclaimed the First Austrian Republic and called a provisional assembly. But after only a short time functioning, the Social-Democratic government proved totally inefficient. The Austrian-German population, disillusioned, abandoned the ancient dream of German unity that their political parties had offered them and, with an eye to practicality, the autonomous development of independent republics appeared to be the most attractive solution. Vienna, a city without an empire, became the capital of hunger and unemployment. At the beginning of 1920, an epidemic of influenza devastated the metropolis. The winter was quite severe and due to a fuel shortage the Viennese were obliged to cut down their forests. In the month of April a gray cloud enveloped the city and an atmosphere of sticky humidity drifted into its streets. The government, incapable of controlling inflation, auctioned off the furniture of the Imperial Palace and rented its rooms to private businesses. An American consortium took advantage of the chaos and offered food in exchange for the Emperor's tapestries. The castle of Schönbrunn was converted into an asylum for orphans, and the wealthy sold off their jewels, antiques and artworks. There instantly appeared a legion of foreign dealers disposed to ransack the city. Public auctions were commonplace and an inappreciable quantity of paintings exited Vienna. Thousands of citizens succumbed to the effects of influenza and hunger.

In the years following the First World War, the fundamental values of European society came crumbling down. A cult of the erotic, including free love and homosexuality, became the fashion in those days. In the most well-known cafés of Vienna — the Central, the Museum and the Herrenhof — an exciting illusion of vitality was being woven, conducive to a culture in which women (who out of necessity had to abandon their former way of life) exercised an unusual degree of promiscuity for the era. "They were never so beautiful, agile and attractive as in those days. The mixture of despair and cynicism," wrote Alfred Polgar, "resulted in a breed of women who were bold and hungry for experiences, obsessed with seizing every minute and disposed to any and all adventures. The coercive social mores were compensated for with a true spirit of escapade. Those tragic times gave birth to an uncontainable and very sensual imagination." These were women who made light of the traditions and abandoned themselves to excesses, longing for the pleasure and hope that had been spoiled in the trenches and on the battlefields. Theirs was the euphoria of survival.

In 1917 there were two women in the cafés who were attracted to Hermann Broch. His restlessness and attentive gaze made an impression on them. The Czech Milena Jasenská and the Austrian Ea von Allesch had renounced the project of founding a family, and had embarked on the adventure of self indulgence. There may have been a touch of cruelty in them, such as is commonly detected in disillusioned women. They were pushing themselves to the limits, as passionate and suicidal as almost all the women who frequented Vienna's cafés in those days.

Hermann Broch met Milena Jasenská in the Café Herrenhof on an autumn afternoon in 1917. She was the daughter of a wealthy family from Prague, ten years younger than he and married to Ernst Pollak. Pollak was a student of philosophy and a militant in the New Erotic Pathways movement, one that preached absolute sexual liberty for single and married individuals alike. The apogee of this movement turned prophecy, and gospel and Pollak's own brand of redemptive philosophy constituted an ephemeral link between the two that ultimately could only be sustained rather faintly during their sporadic encounters. Milena imparted classes of Czech in Vienna and during the summer she helped transport suitcases at the train station. Pollak studied philosophy at the University and he was interested in the work of the Vienna Circle, but he earned no income.

Broch fell in love with Milena and they lived together for several months. She was a sad woman and had a depressive character, "as if she were in the habit of reading six Dostoyevsky novels every day," wrote Franz Blei. Pollak and Broch were dear friends and as time passed he asked Broch to break up with Milena because he was of the conviction that Broch didn't love her. Broch broke off with her immediately without reproaches or accusations. Milena (a name that in Czech means "lover") became the companion of various writers. In 1920 she fell in love with Franz Kafka. She sustained an intimate correspondence with him and upon his death married Ernst Krecjar, a prominent Czech journalist. At one point she dedicated herself passionately to journalism. She worked in a Prague daily and between 1931 and 1937 she was a distinguished militant of the Communist Party. When Kamaniev and Zinoviev were condemned in Moscow, she abandoned the Party and defended the Czech nationalist cause. Milena's passion was distant from Stalinist fanaticism. Her real political affinities were to be found on the other side of the spectrum, closer to the nationalists and Social-Democrats. Her commitment was neither bureaucratic nor sentimental. It had nothing to do with intrigue or redemption. Her temperament led her to the defense of the Jews whom she viewed as victims of barbarity. That same temperament, inseparable from her love of the unfortunate, led her toward the end of her life to participate in the resistance at Ravensbrück death camp, where she died in September of 1944. Hermann Broch thought of her often in the United States. He questioned Pollak about her whereabouts and he referred to her with fondness and admiration. "Milena was an open flame," wrote Franz Kafka, "the likes of which I had never seen before. And at the same time she was sweet, full of spirit, intelligent and entirely committed to self-sacrifice; or perhaps it's more appropriate to say that she thrived on self-sacrifice."

A year later — in June of 1918 — Hermann Broch met Ea von Allesch. The night was hot and humid. Broch invited her to stroll with him along the streets of the city center, and in the darkness in which they found themselves he felt a fervent desire to escape the discomforts of his work in the factory. In that disposition of spirit, he talked to her for hours. Ea recognized his total deliverance to intellectual endeavors, beginning in his adolescence and continuing, undeterred, up to that very night. She learned of his habit of studying with tenacious perseverance, hungry as he was of clarity and critical perspectives. They fell in love and remained together almost a decade (1918-1927). When he separated from Franziska von Rotermann, Broch was twenty eight. His thirties would be dedicated to Ea. But he still remained stuck in the dilemma of a double profession: literature on one side and the textile industry on the other. These two fields were irreconcilable for him. No one at that time exercised such a powerful influence on Broch as Ea von Allesch. He resigned himself to putting an end to the businessman within him, and thanks to her, he discovered that the literary spirit within him possessed much greater force and charm. What were his thoughts at the time? Broch wrote a diary in the form of letters to Ea, and in one of them he confesses his lifelong desire to study philosophy while at the same time explaining that he dreaded universities. "Philosophy has become a science; it needs functionaries and scientific bureaucrats. It is a business, like any other, in which the only requirement is to situate oneself and function. Not even the Chair of the Department should allow himself to become too brilliant. What should one do in this case with one's passion for knowledge? I suspect that an enormous fraud has been committed with the word knowledge. That which philosophy currently produces is nothing more than a record of minutes — anything but knowledge."

Hermann Broch divorced Franziska von Rotermann ten years after their separation and, by March of 1923, he was living periodically in Ea's apartment. Their relationship was one of the hottest items of gossip in the Vienna of the twenties, and one of the most memorable private stories of the Austrian literary scene in the course of the century. In the cafés there was much talk of Broch's triumph over the Baron of

Dirztay, perhaps the most zealous of Ea's suitors, an assiduous client of the Central Café and patron of many writers and artists. Hermann and Ea devoted a passion to their relationship that surpassed their capacity for control. She broke with the strict mores set for high society women at the time and she sought to be an agent of pleasure, to freely love the man whom she had chosen. Nevertheless, she wasn't capable of altering the sternness of her character, which for her seemed to be a means of survival. As corresponded to a woman of her temperament, she had developed a highly ironic intellect, and there was a defect in Ea that even her dearest friends recognized — her proclivity toward detail to the degree of not being able to comprehend events in their totality. Her meticulousness was bothersome to many but it had the advantage of putting Broch's literary vocation to the test. Years later — now in 1949 — Broch would evoke her as: "A women of vast intellectual resources [...] She had an extraordinary sensibility for detail. She was tender and vivacious." In the end her hysteria would destroy her vitality. She was obsessed with the passing of time. Aging horrified her. Perhaps her obsession with aging was accentuated because she lived with Broch, a man eleven years her junior.

"Broch was the first weak man I ever met," wrote Elias Canetti. He wasn't interested in accumulating triumphs or besting others, much less showing off [...] In fact one succumbed to the fascinating gift that he had for listening. His silence made it possible for one to open up to him completely. Never did one trip up against obstacles to honest communication in his presence. One could have said anything to him. Hermann Broch never rejected any subject. One felt uncomfortable in his presence only if one failed to express entirely and completely everything one wished to say."

Canetti met Broch when his relationship with Ea von Allesch was coming to an end. By then she had abandoned all condescendence and she was capable of attacking him pitilessly: "Broch fancies himself a writer," said Ea. "Someone, perhaps a woman, must have planted that unlikely idea in his head. You need only compare his work to that of

Robert Musil to understand that Musil is in fact the real writer. Musil won't allow himself to be deceived by such nonsense as Freudian theory, while Broch is a slave to Freudian superstitions, imagining that it is possible to be reborn."

The Angel of The Sleepwalkers

Unlike the other Austrian writers of his generation, Hermann Broch was a staunch believer in psychoanalysis. In the autumn of 1927, after his reentrance to the University, he made friends with various members of the Psychoanalytic Association of Vienna, above all with August Aichorn (Freud's pupil), Hedwig Schaxel and Willie Hoffer. After some months, Dr. Schaxel had become his psychoanalyst. His therapy program consisted of thrice weekly sessions over the course of nearly eight years. Broch thought it was important to explain his childhood in order to understand how his father's homosexuality had incurred on his development. Psychoanalysis taught him how not to confuse his emotions, how to put things in perspective and how to recognize his own strength. Nevertheless, Broch wasn't totally satisfied with his experience: "My analysis in Vienna was deficient. It was only much later, in New York, that Paul Federn revealed to me the true power of psychoanalysis. This is not to say that I am unappreciative of Dr. Schaxel's intervention. Before beginning therapy with him I was a terribly insecure person. I couldn't finish any of my books; much less publish them. Despite his inability to assist me in resolving certain conflicts, I confess that I owe my life to Dr. Hedwig Schaxel." In 1927 Hermann Broch decided to end his indentured servitude to the family enterprises. He accepted the proposal of his friend Felix Wolf, selling him the factory of fabrics and textiles. Wolf paid $100,000 for them, a significant sum in those days. The money was divided up in equal parts among the members of his family. Broch kept very little for himself. Franziska and his son received the larger part of it, which by law corresponded entirely to him. The timing of this move could not have been better, since Broch sold his assets not long before the stock market crash of 1929.

At age forty, Broch returned to the University of Vienna and enrolled as an auditor. During the twenties, the Department of Philosophy, completely under the dominion of the Vienna Circle, was an entity of unique character in Austrian history. Professor Moritz Schlick (1882-1936), founder and critic of the Circle, had accomplished the assembly of an extraordinary group of theoreticians specializing in logic, physics and mathematics. They held their meetings on Thursday evenings. The most prominent members were Otto Neurath, Rudolf Carnap, Herbert Feigl, Friederich Waismann, Victor Kraft, Karl Popper; the psychoanalyst Heinz Hartmann, the jurist Felix Kaufmann and the mathematicians Kurt Gödel and Karl Menger. Schlick maintained, moreover, a tight working relationship with Ludwig Wittgenstein. The theoreticians of the Circle were rigorous and had imposed on themselves a strict rule. They valued scientific precision above all things. They believed in logic and in the natural sciences. They understood logical propositions to be of an analytical-tautological character, whereas those of empirical science, "true" science, were synthetic and referred exclusively to the facts. Nothing may be affirmed regarding the relationship between these two realms because such propositions would be neither synthetic-empirical nor logical-analytical. The theoreticians of the Vienna Circle were extremely adverse to metaphysical premises and contemporary analytical philosophy is firmly rooted in their perspectives. The relationship between empirical formulations and the facts should be subject to verification. The propositions of empirical science must correspond to experience, and to that end, certain fundamental propositions were crafted which enabled them to more carefully observe and register reality.

Broch attended the lectures and seminars of Moritz Schlick. At first he wanted to get a doctorate but he was impeded by the lack of an undergraduate degree. During this period Broch debated with the theoreticians of logical empiricism. Rudolf Carnap analyzed in his classes the nonsense of metaphysical formulations and the limits of philosophy.

Schlick discussed the difference between life and knowledge. Phillip Frank, the physicist, assured his students that the constancy of material phenomena should occupy the center of their attention and investigations. And then there was Otto Neurath who was seeking a mathematical model of truth. "From the ethical perspective," noted Broch, "analytical philosophy could be considered anything but philosophy." Nevertheless, Broch was a firm believer in the affirmations of Ludwig Wittgenstein, who held that art and literature were the spaces where the central theme of philosophy, the question of life's meaning, could and should be legitimately clarified.

The moment in which Hermann Broch decided to write his first novel coincided with the final phase of Europe's decline. Night was falling and the world was going to sleep; but he remained as a man who has awoken in the middle of the night. There was a kind of fairy godmother behind each one of his forays into the genre of the novel. Anna Herzog was the angel behind *The Sleepwalkers*. Previously, he had been with Ea von Allesch, and his equilibrium and sobriety contrasted with her fury and angst. Anna Herzog, fifteen years younger than Broch, was born in Malczka, a town in Czechoslovakia. She was an intelligent woman, discreet and attractive. When Broch began drafting *The Sleepwalkers*, she corrected the manuscript several times. On the heels of an exhausting relationship with Ea von Allesch, Broch had succumbed to lethargy. Anna Herzog offered him love and pleasure devoid of exigencies. Accepting that she would never be his bride, she conceived of her devotion to Broch as the fulfillment of a dream. Anna was direct and maternal, her frankness and rectitude captivated Hermann Broch. It seems that her lack of affectation was a function of her resigned melancholy. She displayed both common and prodigious qualities. She read Broch's works with profuse passion, always informing him of her doubts and disagreements. She never shrank before his erudition, nor did she allow herself to be overwhelmed by his intellect. Her love for Broch was exclusive and unequaled.

As Hitler rose to power, Anna recalled that Broch was Jewish. She foresaw with greater clarity and sooner than Broch the coming holocaust. She rightly interpreted the political programs of the Führer as the hallucinations of an infirm mind: Vienna would become the tomb of the Jews. She left Austria in March of 1938 as a consequence of her discernments. She lived awhile in Paris and later in Mexico. She rightly understood what was to come. Her friends suffered jail, exile and countless miseries. But what was it that Anna was seeking in Mexico? She had come to loathe life in Europe: this is how she put it in a letter to Broch, to whom she never ceased writing. Anna Herzog died in 1980 in a small apartment in the neighborhood of Tacubaya in western Mexico City. We know nothing of her life in this city, nor the place in which her body was buried.

A New Moral Space

Broch began writing *The Sleepwalkers* in 1927. The project consumed five years of his life. "My novel supposes literature to be a space where the problems rejected by contemporary science and philosophy — unable to find space for it in their rationalist conceptions — may be discussed. [...] In fact I contend that literature is quite capable of addressing many essential problems which science, in its lumbering and methodical pursuit of progress, has utterly failed to detect." The modern novel assumes in Broch the critical inheritance of Western thought, a tradition that begins with Plato and concludes with Nietzsche. *The Sleepwalkers* renews the treatment and exploration of traditional themes related to metaphysics: What reasons do we have to live? Why and for what do we live? Certainly some passages of the novel give the impression that Broch is actually a philosopher disguised as a novelist, a theoretician who takes advantage of the genre to intercalate fragments of his personal philosophy of history. There is every indication that he was aware of this tendency in his writings, He was highly critical of his literary abilities and at times he thought of himself as a novelist without imagination, without narrative power. Nevertheless, the important thing in his view was that his novels should capture the degradation of values inherent in his époque. Such is the critical impulse that lies behind his perspectives on Berlin at the end of the nineteenth century, exemplified in his portrayals of cultural malaise and his rendering of the erotic expression of unconscious conflicts. Broch's intention wasn't simply to retell or recreate the historical reality of his times, rather to apprehend and critique it as well: which may explain why, even as a novelist, he frequently displays the qualities of a philosopher or cultural critic. His zest for life was coupled with his passion for literature, an unfortunate passion in light of what he suffered for his vocation.

Friedrich Schlegel, referring to the continual interplay between the intellectual and narrative discourses within the novel, claimed that a novel should always function potentially as a theory of the novel. Broch holds fast to this doctrine, as he gambles on the powers of literary revelation. *The Sleepwalkers* is actually a trilogy imbedded in successive yet distinct time periods: 1888, *Passenow or Romanticism* / 1903, *Esch or Anarchy* / 1918, *Hugenau or Objectivity*. These narratives mark the first occasion in which Broch transposes the focus of his attention from Vienna and the Viennese to German places and people.

Turn of the century Berlin, a world of wealthy landowners and Prussian military officials, constitutes the atmosphere in whose center appears lieutenant Joachim von Passenow. Without realizing it Passenow has lost faith in traditional values. His brother died in a duel. "He died upholding our honor," says his father, repeatedly. Joachim, plagued by insecurities, embraces the waning forms of the past. Fitted in his military uniform, he becomes the symbol of an attitude of reverence that, according to Broch, was characteristic of the romantic period. At this point two destabilizing forces enter the picture: Eduard von Bertrand, an aristocrat who abandoned the army and considers the traditional customs and sentiments to be merely atavistic residues, representations of conservatism and stupidity, and Ruzena, a young prostitute characterized by uneasiness and spurred on by carnal appetites, a precarious woman, complex and pitiable. Joachim falls in love with Ruzena, though he denies his sentiments. Ruzena is the definition of anarchy and corruption, a kind of "Lulú," capable of anything. Her contrary is Elizabeth, the genteel daughter of a wealthy neighbor. Joachim perceives her as a symbol of purity, an angelic herald. When he discovers that Bertrand is in love with her, he decides to marry her. The last scene of *Passenow or Romanticism* is quite definitive: Joachim lies in bed with Elizabeth, now his wife, still dressed in his uniform. The ridiculous presence of the uniform and the gross mythologization of romantic tropes within the narrative highlight the farcical quality of his existence. Joachim is a sleep-walker: incapable of truly believing in or affirming anything, a simulator of graciousness and reconciliation.

Edmund Wilson assures us that the abstractions of German philoso-phy — seemingly coarse or obscure when translated into English or French — when expressed in the original German, with the sturdiness of its capital letters, create the impression of the voice of primitive gods. As a matter of fact the word *Schlafwandler* (sleepwalkers) denotes the tribe that traverses the land of dreams, those who have renounced real-ity. When one considers this somnambulant state against the backdrop of a corrupt and authoritarian society, the political implications become clear.

While writing *Esch or Anarchy* Broch perceived the germs of inse-curity and submission that transformed the petty bourgeoisie into an unconditional ally of fascism. Esch, a bookkeeper, loses his job without any explanation. Although he finds another quite easily, he begins to find fault with all aspects of reality. He is incapable of thought and action beyond the categories of "Must" and "Ought." True knowledge is denied him. Esch is a professional informer, something of a spy. He might pose as a militant of some radical party, a member of a religious sect or a corrupt union leader. "The gamut of passions that dominate the bloody history of our century," writes Milan Kundera, "may be found implicit, unmasked, diagnosed and dreadfully visible in his modest adventures."

Esch falls in love with a widow, Mrs. Hentjen, who waitresses in a bar. He discovers sexuality in her company, transforming her into an ob-ject of erotic adoration, and they plan to emigrate to the United States together. There is actually no one less attractive, erotic or exciting than Mrs. Hentjen. But Esch, hostage to his sexual pulsations, gets caught up in a world of alcoholics, whores and pimps. He organizes wrestling matches between women and he deceives and cheats the spectators. Despite his morally questionable behavior, the search for a guilty party within the narrative discourse proves futile. Meanwhile, we learn of Eduard von Bertrand, a powerful industrialist who lives in a castle and is a homosexual. Esch seeks him out and finds him. Bertrand bears the mark of evil in his face. Esch denounces him. He marries Mrs. Hentjen and Bertrand commits suicide.

The last of the sleepwalkers is an assassin. Hugenau, an unscrupulous opportunist, is more implacable and shifting, more alive than the value systems that pretend to contain him. The setting is a small city of the military zone and Esch is the owner of the local newspaper. Passenow and Esch possess a similar mentality, that of the religious and military factions. They may be reduced to these two perspectives with all the risks of such an excessive simplification, but it is hardly a stretch to affirm that they represent the dogmatic postures that people tend to assume before the inscrutable face of reality. Hugenau, on the other hand, is a tireless worker. He takes over Esch's newspaper, becomes a businessman, corners Passenow, and, upon the eruption of the revolution of 1918, he blindsides and assassinates Esch. He then persecutes and subdues Mrs. Hentjen and abandons the city, accompanied by Passenow, who slips into delirium and loses his mind. After the war Hugenau steals Mrs. Hutjen's fortune and transforms himself into an honorable head of a household, an exemplary citizen. Hugenau is the executioner in a world that has condemned itself, an individual devoid of memory and remorse. The progressive degradation of his values, whose principal victims are Esch and Passenow, crystallizes in various sections that count among the best of twentieth-century German literature. Some of the most memorable sections include the one about the bricklayer Ludwig Gödicke, whose life was accidentally saved in the trenches, permitting him to gradually regain consciousness; and that of lieutenant Jaretzki, lame and alcoholic, wielding his sarcasm like a weapon in the face of a world which shows him no quarter; and the story of the doctors at the military hospital, increasingly aware of the meaninglessness of their efforts; and that of Hanna Wendling, one of the most convincing characters in the novel who, by taking her own life, embraces the principle of uncertainty.

The narrative axis of *The Sleepwalkers* is ultimately the lost identity of its characters, related to the collapse of European civilization. It is virtually the same argument Sigmund Freud advances in *Civilization and its Discontents*, whereby that which civilization is not able to incorporate or assimilate turns against it and destroys it. *Hugenau or Objectivity* is the most complex, dark and bitter of all Broch's work. Its difficulty resides principally in its form. He chose to narrate the love story of a young lady from the Salvation Army in sonnets, while theoretical digressions on the degradation of values continually interrupt the plot. His editor, Brody, pleaded with him to minimize the theoretical content, but Broch refused to cut it out because he was convinced that he had achieved "a new moral space" within the genre of the novel.

The Sleepwalkers was a critical success. Thomas Mann noted in May of 1932: "During the last few months I have been reading Herman Broch's trilogy. I am convinced that it is a significant work, rich and appealing, and that with time it will hold great importance among us." However, in February of 1933, the triumph of the Nazis dashed the hopes of a market in Germany. Most of the books never left the warehouse and not even the production costs were recuperated. "*The Sleepwalkers*, my friend," wrote Broch's editor, "certainly brought you prestige, but not riches."

The Ruins of Red Vienna

In March of 1933 the British Secret Service reported on the situation in Austria: "Here in Vienna rumors are spreading about a *coup d'état*. It seems that Chancellor Dollfuss is trying to push back the date for elections. The national economy is in ruins. It is estimated that there are more than four hundred thousand unemployed. The railway workers' strikes have paralyzed the country. Despite the tenseness and instability, there is absolutely no indication that there may be a Nazi upsurge in Austria. Dollfuss combats the Social-Democrats and the Nazis with equal vigor." Some days later, the president of Parliament renounced his post, citing a procedural altercation. Dollfuss took advantage of the occasion to dissolve Parliament, and before the Supreme Court could pronounce its decision, he also dissolved the Judiciary. Thereafter he closed two major newspapers, limited freedom of expression, instated the death penalty and jailed his most visible political enemies. Through his alliance with Mussolini, Dollfuss believed he could confront Adolf Hitler. He never suspected that this alliance was a trap. Armed nationalist groups known as *Heimwehren*, a sort of paramilitary police organization, urged the government to establish Nazism in Austria.

Under the circumstances, Engelbert Dollfuss should have foreseen that such widespread working-class resistance might give rise to a virulent *coup d'état*, which is what happened on February 12, 1934, when groups of the League of Republican Protection clashed with the police in Linz. The Social-Democrats called a general strike and the next morning armed contingents assaulted the troops of the army. Dollfuss, attempting to prove his political control to the Germans, ordered the razing of

"Red Vienna," the working-class neighborhood of the city. Throughout more than three days, the army bombarded the streets and edifices of the zone and executed all prisoners. Dollfuss wanted to avert the rise and propagation of Nazism in Austria. His own brand of Austro-Fascism, however, was not up to the task. Dollfuss was a politician without a following, an ideologist without a program. No one really knew what the term "New Austria" meant, and his rhetoric of a return to Christian tradition was neither comprehensible nor compelling to the masses. While his companions in the Christian Social Party lamented the fate of the nation, he gambled on a Catholic utopia financed with the help of the Church. Unfortunately the one-time political realist was now becoming a kind of illuminated inquisitor. The police and the nationalist bands that tortured Social-Democrat workers in Vienna's jails were the executioners of his Holy Inquisition. Dollfuss' plan was quick in meeting its demise. Here was a politician who never invoked the masses and constantly invoked God. Here was a Catholic Church that supported him only in order to preserve its own grip on power. Here was a citizenry tired of insensitive decisions being made in the seat of power: a population which languished in misery and was always disposed to submit itself to a small radical minority eager for martyrdom. Dollfuss' error was his incredible ingenuousness.

His government crumbled under the weight of the circumstances. He was apparently unaware that his policies were actually benefiting his executioners: The civil war had liquidated Social-Democracy, destroyed Republican institutions and given power to paramilitary groups. Dollfuss succumbed to the same violence he had hoped to exorcise. On July 25, 1934, a National-Socialist agitator named Otto Planetta, intending to provoke a *coup d'état*, shot him in the head. The ideologists of Austro-Fascism were redeemed four years later, in March of 1938, when the Nazis occupied the country.

Another Austrian ideology, Austro-Marxism, had been buried on February 12, 1934, among the ruins of "Red Vienna." For over twenty years its theoreticians insisted that the abolition of the structures of injustice would not guarantee the advent of the reign of liberty. They signaled the incongruence of "proletarian internationalism," they resisted submitting themselves to simplistic Manichean schemes and they dedicated themselves to the revision of Marxist theory so that it might serve as a source of enrichment to democracy. Austro-Marxism demanded the critique of the false myths of socialist theory, citing the danger that any foreseeable liberty could become too easily foiled, co-opted and crippled in the structures of the "new religion." Changing a society's economic order, said Otto Bauer, in no way guaranteed that democracy and liberty would flourish, just as establishing a democratic government wouldn't necessarily guarantee equality and justice for all.

The Vertigo of Algebra

Hermann Broch frequently turned his pen to political essays. His essays incarnate the heritage and continuity of European culture and recall the best of this tradition. Starting from his first foray into the genre, "Constitutional Dictatorship and Democracy in the Workers' Councils" (1919), Broch argued that one had to come to terms with the political circumstances as the mathematician comes to terms with the physical laws of space. In another of his essays, he wrote: "The effects of the breeze on a rose reveals to us from which of the four corners of the world the winds of history are blowing. In heaven *justice constitutes power*, in purgatory *power constitutes injustice*, and in hell *injustice constitutes power*. In our daily life here on earth, however, *power constitutes justice*. Though we must always contend with the presence of the devil, we may also count on the anticipation of paradise. But the miracle will not happen unless we work toward its advent. The miracle where *justice constitutes power* requires, first of all, that justice has been conferred the power to accomplish this task."

His abandonment of socialist utopianism led him to embrace democracy as a sister to liberty. He believed that we should recuperate Kant's neglected conviction in which he holds that the people are more curious, intelligent and reasonable than their representatives presume. There is no reason to relegate the people to underage status. The demolition of false ideological certitudes would herald a new beginning.

His novel *The Sleepwalkers* was a commercial failure, and worse still, it heightened his disenchantment with literature: an obsession that haunted Hermann Broch until the day of his death. During the thirties he evolved rapidly toward staunch theoretical positions, for example, his confidence in redemption through logos rather than through the natural sciences. His philosophical inclinations led his literary work into the realm of metaphysics and ethics. He understood that the experience of anarchy and meaninglessness in modernity was due, above all, to the degradation of universal values. This verdict had much in common with the Christian critique of modernity. Rather than advancing a particularly scientific theory, through his writings Broch posited an aesthetic hope of constructing from the most contradictory elements a significant theory of values. The Vienna Circle had no use for this sort of neo-Platonism. With Wittgenstein, for example, philosophy had reached the level that other disciplines (such as poetry, music and painting) had reached before: a fusion with its own critique, a suspicion of its own impossibilities.

Jürgen Habermas has observed that at the beginning of the twentieth century philosophical deliberation suffered ruptures very similar to those of painting in its movement toward abstraction, music in its movement toward a dodecaphonic system, and literature as it abandoned the traditional forms of narration. In Broch we detect a strange yet revealing contradiction. His highly experimental narratives *Hugenau or Objectivity*, and, ten years later, *The Death of Virgil* utterly shattered the idea of the traditional novel, and yet he actually espoused a return to something like the traditional Platonic vision of the world.

One of the most disquieting of Broch's ideas is condensed in the title of his essay, "Life Without the Platonic Idea" (1932): "The concept of redemption finds itself very deeply rooted in the human race. However, redemption from death can only be achieved in the realm of the spirit, nowadays rarely appreciated. No one knows if future philosophical inquiries will find a home in mathematical logic, or if they will be relegated to literary forms. Freedom in society is born of the combat between political dictatorships and the Platonic ideal; and while in this earthly combat the Platonic ideal and redemption would appear to be defeated, it shouldn't be forgotten that philosophy did not only follow religion but it also anteceded it. In the realm of the spirit, Platonic ideals and freedom have always triumphed. Freedom finds itself chained to reason."

The publication of "Evil within the Value System of Art" (1933), "James Joyce and the Present" (1936) and "Cosmogony of the Novel" (1936) provoked numerous criticisms about the philosophical preoccupations in Broch's writings. Despite the prestige he won with *The Sleepwalkers* and his essays, outside of literary circles very few people knew of him. Around the mid-thirties he had become what the English refer to as "an author's author," a writer appreciated by his colleagues and few others. "The Viennese were chiefly interested in spectacle and calumny," wrote Heinz Politzer. "In those days they could have cared less about an intellectual who lived as an austere monk."

Broch understood the lessons of James Joyce. In various respects he was of a similar temperament as the Irish novelist, though less hermetic. James Joyce had accomplished, said Broch, that which Goethe had accomplished in *Wilhelm Meister's Apprenticeship*, capturing in a work of literature the totality of an époque. His essay on Joyce is a critique of his methodology. Broch was fascinated by the impetus of describing sixteen hours of life in one thousand two hundred pages, which amounts to seventy-five pages per hour, more than a page per minute, almost a line per second. His interest in Joyce had less to do with Joyce's outlook on life than with his methodology: "The mere succession of things becomes a unifying principal: the process of transformation into a unity of the simultaneous." *Ulysses* gave him the necessary perspective to write *The Death of Virgil*, a novel in which for over five hundred thirty-three pages Broch narrates the most uncommon of days, that of a man's death.

In "Cosmogony of the Novel" he takes up the task of tracing the most notable differences between kitsch and art. Broch was after an ethical distinction: "If there exist moral exigencies in art — and a brief stroll through our artistic circles should be enough to convince anyone that they are indeed necessary — they should be formulated in the manner of prohibitions: 'One should not imitate in part or whole other works of art, for in this case one will create kitsch'; or 'One should not work with an inordinate concern for the results, for in this case one will create kitsch'; and finally, 'One should not confuse the work of art with adherence to dogmatic principles for the production of said work, for in this case one will certainly produce kitsch.' One who produces kitsch is not one whose production is an inferior kind of art, nor one who is partially or totally ignorant of art, for such a person cannot be measured according to the standards of aesthetics, rather we must accept — now, as you may have guessed, we find ourselves in the realm of talking films and operetta — that we are definitely dealing with a morally degraded person, a delinquent with evil inclinations and no scruples. Or, to put in less pathetic terms, such a person is decidedly a pig. And we draw this conclusion based on the fact that kitsch represents evil within the realm of art. Would you prefer an archetypal example of kitsch? Nero playing his lute before the bodies of Christians enveloped in flames: He is the archetypal dilettante, an authentic esthete who sacrifices everything in his intent to create an aesthetic effect. The true artist, on the contrary, is not concerned with sublime effects. His only concern is diligence."

There is a drop of kitsch in all art because there is a minimum of convention in all art, that is, a necessity to provoke pleasure in the public, and no artist is exempt from this quality. As we recover and recreate the heroic epic, the novel may degenerate into a pyrotechnic game of Neronian character whose vision satisfies the distinct impulses of the author and the reader due to their emotional identification with the hero. From *Don Quixote* to the contemporary detective novel, the novelistic genre represents a world of conquerors that is renewed and updated time and time again. "Whether it is the erotic hero of *Dangerous Liaisons* by Choderlos de Laclos, the characters of Ernest Hemingway (Nick Carter, pitted against the delinquents of the underworld), the magician Bolsa Saccard of Emile Zola, or the Man without Qualities of Robert Musil, we are always dealing with a heroic epic very near to kitsch." The producer of kitsch remains trapped in a system of partial values in whose center beauty is to be found as the supreme value. As Broch saw it, only Joyce, Kafka and Gide had produced works of literature which also stood as radical critiques of literature.

When Robert Musil read "Evil within the Value-System of Art," he believed that it plagiarized his own ideas. In October of 1933, he noted in his diary: "While not necessarily constituting a conscious act of plagiarism, there appears to be an unacknowledged source behind Hermann Broch's arguments. If one repeatedly rubs up against a white wall it is only natural that one should find one's suit stained all over with white spots." He wrote Broch a letter lamenting that he didn't mention him, to which Broch replied: "The veiled accusation that I omitted your name in order to highlight or exaggerate the originality of my insights, let us speak frankly, is incredible. You might as well accuse me of blatant plagiarism [...] I have followed your struggles with literature for many years now [...] and my admiration for your work will not diminish, no matter what you may think of my own. In "Cosmogony of the Novel" I cite *The Man Without Qualities* to illustrate my central thesis, more so than any other contemporary novel." There is a certain irony in this response, because *The Man Without Qualities* appears in "Cosmogony of the Novel" as the most intelligent and subtle example of kitsch. Robert Musil responded some time later. Refraining from a lengthy discussion of their conflict, he simply states: "I thank you for your generous clarifications, though I am afraid that our points of view are irreconcilable. I would also like you to know that my objections were not intended to subtract value or autonomy from your work."

In his tastes, sensibility and perspectives on literature, Musil was a very different writer from Broch. He proved to be very reserved with respect to Broch's work. He never bothered either to admire it or detract from its merit. When Franz Blei sent him a summary of *The Sleepwalkers*, Musil consigned in his diaries: "His projects seem a bit like my own [...] but Broch's handling of the 'philosophical novel' is rather suspect. I am convinced that he is incorrect, mistaken. If I enter into the discussion I would have to challenge him on philosophical grounds, or on the contrary, attack him personally."

In the thirties, Broch saw Musil as the most pathetic example of the unsuccessful writer, cornered by economic penuries and without a future of which to speak. Although they conversed on a few occasions, they were never really friends. Broch's vision was vaster though not necessarily more profound than that of Musil. Broch, for example, foresaw the advent of the totalitarian politics incarnated in the figure of Adolf Hitler, who exercised his dominion thanks to the delirium of the masses. His Jewish condition led him to always ask himself about "the other," about the existence of "the others." He had a clear consciousness about the disparity between the Jewish and the Austrian cultures. Musil's "failure" terrified him. It was the expression of the ruin of literary dreams and aspirations. Still, in the end they were united in a common misfortune, powerless to avoid it. During his exile in the United States Hermann Broch would experience scantiness and miseries comparable to those of Robert Musil.

One of the greatest of Broch's lessons was the way in which he sought to bring literature to the world. In the decade of the thirties, he initiated his career in theater with *The Expiation* (1932), *The Business Affairs of Baron Laborde* (1934), *It All Remains the Same* (1934) and *Only in One's Dreams* (1934). In March of 1934, Gustav Hartung, one of the best men of the theater in Germany, staged *The Expiation*. The play was premiered in the Schauspielhaus Theater of Zurich, but it was only on the bill for a few weeks and it disappeared without achieving much distinction. All of Hermann Broch's plays betray the presence of a novelist who narrates his stories and hides from the spectator the true significance of the dramatic action. They are basically verbal manifestations of a textual narrative. Nevertheless, they are governed by the same psychological and artistic necessity that led Broch to create his other characters. *The Expiation*, his best work, is the clearest example of this phenomenon. Herbert Filsmann — the protagonist and a character with whom Broch was obsessed — would become, on another occasion, the centerpiece of an unfinished novel. The young executive attempts to save his factories from ruin. He negotiates with the labor unions, fights against a great consortium, confides in a friend who betrays him and ultimately commits suicide. Herbert Filsmann never achieved the stature of Broch's other characters, such as those who populated *Passenow or Hugenau*.

The thirties were years of furious production for Broch, and not only in theater plays. It was as if he were disposed to recover all the lost time he had lost. In 1933 he wrote the six short stories of *Circle of Animals*, along with the essays "Theology, Positivism and Literature," "On the Problem of Knowledge in Music," "Myth and Literature in Thomas Mann," and a book of poetry, *Patmos*. From July to November he wrote *The Unknown Quantity*, a novel that Fischer Press published in December. None of his other books earned him as much money as this one: five thousand Swiss francs, plus another payment for some articles he would write for *Vossische Zeitung*, a Berlin newspaper. It tells the story of Richard Hieck, a young mathematician obsessed with the idea of pure knowledge. Hieck finds in mathematics a road toward perfection, the modern version of the mystical life, the gospel of equations and calculations. These eternal longings are opposed to what might be termed his temporal ones, those of the passions and the emotions, constituting an alternative form of knowledge. Richard Hieck clings to rational and scientific knowledge. He pretends to control life from the dominion of mathematics, but the death of his brother returns him to reality. Skeptical with respect to nearly all things in those days, Broch was equally ambivalent with respect to one of his greatest passions: mathematics.

On February 19, 1937, the young Argentine writer Jorge Luis Borges reviewed *The Unknown Quantity* for *Hogar* magazine in Buenos Aires. "A woman regretted, at dusk, that we couldn't dream the same dream: 'How beautiful it would be to dream that I was traveling through a labyrinth in Egypt with you, and the next day, upon alluding to the dream, not only would you remember it, but you would recall some detail which I had missed and which might help explain the dream's significance or else intensify its mystery.' I praised this very elegant desire of hers and we spoke of the competition that such dreams, shared by thousands of couples, would offer to reality. (Only afterward did I realize that these hypothetical 'shared' dreams do in fact exist, for reality itself is such a dream). In *The Unknown Quantity*, the conflict doesn't take place between the real facts and the dreamed ones, rather between the real ones and the lucid and vertiginous universe of algebra. The hero, Richard Heick, is a mathematician 'for whom everyday life isn't important' — much the same as our Almafuerte — and whose true world is that of symbols. The narrator doesn't limit himself to simply telling us that he is a mathematician. He introduces us to his world and makes us familiar with its trials and immaculate victories [...] His younger brother's suicide restores Hieck to 'reality,' a balanced orb in which all the faculties of man cohabitate. Ultimately, we are grateful that such a decisive revelation wasn't triggered by a gypsy's fortune or by the charm of Marlene Dietrich. I suspect, however, that I would have much rather enjoyed the inverse argument, one in which we witnessed the progressive invasion of the commonplace world by the Platonic world of symbols."

On October 14, 1934, Joseph Broch died, elderly and aged. "Two weeks before his death we signed a truce," wrote Hermann Broch. "I was confirmed in my belief that underneath it all my father was a good and generous soul." Broch was to administer the inheritance and upon his mother's death he was to take possession of the assets. His brother Fritz opposed this with all the measures at his disposal. They took their dispute to the courts. They hired lawyers and fought it out for three years. Elias Canetti has provided what is perhaps the most intimate portrait of Broch in those days: "As he sat before me I could see him well in the light. The way he was seated impressed me. His bird-like head was a little sunken into his shoulders [...] His eyes, if they could breathe, gave the impression of holding their breath [...] He possessed a beautiful fragility whereby he seemed to be dependent on the happenings, relations and oscillations of the people around him. Many would be of the opinion that this was a weakness. But I have a right to call it what I will. I maintain that a weakness of which one is entirely conscious constitutes a strength or even a virtue."

Writing is Knowing

On June 22, 1936, professor Moritz Schlick traversed the central patio of the University of Vienna, as he did on all Mondays, and he approached the famed "Staircase of the Philosophers," on his way to his classroom. It was nine in the morning. As he was going up and conversing with one of his young female students, a man of some thirty-five years, wearing glasses and dressed in black, passed quickly by his side and four steps higher he spun around, took out a revolver and shot him in the heart. Professor Schlick raised his arms, let out a scream and collapsed on the stairs. The assassin exclaimed: "Rot in hell!"

The murderer, Dr. Johann Nelböck, was an old student of Schlick's. Eleven months later, during the trial, he declared that he had executed the professor as a means of social prophylactics:

"Schlick believed in the reduction of human experience to only that which is perceptible — Nelböck complained — and he upheld carnal pleasure as the exclusive basis of life. Any kind of religious sentiment was totally absurd in his view. Schlick ruined my life. He destroyed my affections and fouled my relationships."

The dispute between Schlick and Nelböck was well publicized, yet the jury only heard the lamentations of the murderer. Nelböck knew quite well what to say to the representatives of "New Austria." He struck a chord that resonated with the tradition of Catholic authoritarianism. Nelböck accused the professor of having "intimate relations" with a female student and he denounced him as a social delinquent. He was condemned to nine years of prison but four years later, in October of 1938, he was pardoned for lack of evidence. The murder of Moritz Schlick was not so much a consequence of the conduct of one paranoid individual as it was symptomatic of the climate of intolerance and persecution that reigned in Austria. For Hermann Broch it was the first sign of alarm, the first warning that he should leave Vienna.

Subsequently, he took refuge in the countryside: Baden and Laxemburg. Munich and Tyrol were also the sites of his retreat. He deployed his intellectual force in two directions: *Demeter or Bewitchment*, a new novel, and the "Resolution of the League of Nations." Daniel Brody, one of his best friends and his editor, advised him to forget about politics and return to his novels. Contrary to the criticisms, Broch wasn't trying to reform his contemporaries, only to highlight the situation of human rights in Europe and to convoke a sort of permanent commission. As with many of his essays, the "Resolution of the League of Nations" remained in the drawers of his desk. At various times in the course of those years Broch's spirit waned. After *The Sleepwalkers*, should he continue on the path of the literary vanguard? Or should he not turn to a form of writing that would be more functional? His books were not selling well and the laudatory opinions of the critics and the prestige he had garnered didn't translate into money in his pocket. "I am two chapters into my next novel," he noted. "Writing is a means of knowing, and in literature, knowledge is derived through form. New knowledge can only be obtained through new forms. Yet such a process requires distancing oneself from one's readership, not selling books and setting off on a path that Joyce exhausted years ago. The more one experiments with form the more one distances oneself from functional writing, and from the possibility of selling books. It wouldn't be much of a dilemma, however, if I hadn't presently such a need for money."

The presence of Anna, daughter of Gustav and Alma Mahler-Werfel, the afternoons they spent in the cafes and their passionate conversations, helped lighten the years he lived leading up to the First World War. Anna and Broch had humorously agreed to marry when she turned eighty and he one hundred. New friendships granted him the favor of consolation and confidence: Ernst Bloch, Elias Canetti, Alban Berg and the sculptor Fritz Wotruba. By that time, however, the family's fortune had run out, the courses offered in the cultural centers of the Social-Democrats were suspended, and the newspaper articles he wrote hardly provided him enough for a meal in a second-class restaurant. No one was less prepared to earn a living as a writer than this fragile intellectual who, as Hannah Arendt had noticed, was stubbornly convinced that the importance of a novelist may be measured by the obstacles he places before his readers, the resistance he offers with respect to surrendering himself to even one of his readers.

In some passages of his letters, Broch alludes to the past fifty years in Austrian history as an era in which Austrians demonstrated an astonishing incompetence at resolving their problems. Once the religious exit had expired, the major political movements of the twentieth century set about transforming themselves into substitutes of religion. The redemptive prophecies and obsessions incarnated exemplarily in Nazism and Marxism-Leninism (the dominion of the masses) was not an abstraction, rather it was a reality in Germany and in the Soviet Union. Hermann Broch's insistence in considering these political ideologies as religious doctrines is the most evident and constant characteristic in his late essays. The same is true of his novel, *Bewitchment,* which constitutes a brilliant critique of Nazism and the delirium of the masses.

In *Bewitchment,* the narrator, a rural doctor in a mountain village, recalls the events when a foreigner, Marius Ratti, appeared one day to initiate his public life and assume a position of power in the community. Another character, Mrs. Gisson, a wise woman and folk healer by profession, opposes the demagogy of the "prophet" and loses her life. While in the beginning the inhabitants of the village ignore and despise Ratti, after a few months the young fall under his spell, succumbing to his mystical ideas (centered on the sacred character of the land), his triumphant sermons and his charismatic presence. Then things take an unexpected twist. The landowners attempt to manipulate his magical powers, taking advantage of him in order to liquidate their political adversaries. At this point, mystical obsessions, mythological images and pagan rituals abound in the story. The community comes to believe the most absurd legends, reinventing the history of their village. Some even change their names and biographies. Finally, during some Catholic festivities, there is an eruption of sadistic violence. A terrifying desire of vengeance takes possession of everyone and they murder Mrs. Gisson. The doctor, who participates in and narrates the deeds, is also a victim of this collective delirium.

According to George Steiner, *Bewitchment*, one of the great novels of the twentieth century, is possibly more penetrating and efficacious than Thomas Mann's *Doctor Faust*. From the literary perspective, both works intend to reveal the psychological and social roots of Hitlerism. The implications of *Bewitchment* are multifold. Among the most important qualities of the novel are: (1) its profound exploration of mythical-religious phenomena and (2) its astute exposure of the inferno of modern culture, even extending beyond the matter of Austria and the Nazi period. It was at this time that Broch published his essay, "The Death of Culture" (1935), whose central obsession was the suspicion of the impossibility of art: "From the caves of Altamira to the works of Beethoven and Goethe, artists have preserved the capacity to transform reality into images [...] In our times this capacity may be disappearing."

As he was writing *Bewitchment* he began to have doubts, once again, as to the purpose of literature. Reduced to solitude in the mountains of Tyrol and surrounded by the books of the Church fathers — Saint Agustin, Dionysus Areopagita, St. Irineus and St. John Crisostomo — he noted: "We writers know nothing about creation, we do not create works of art. We work. Our work consists of writing phrases and words that may have passed some ten times through our consciousness, ten or even one hundred times, it doesn't matter, for we are only conscious to the degree that we have assumed each one of those words, integrating them into our hearts [...] One must not neglect the supreme commandment of the novelist — rigor [...] The novelist who contemplates his novel as a work of art is condemned to vanish. Flaubert and Stendhal left behind a mere spasm [...] Even Joyce's legacy, for all his efforts, won't amount to much more than a spasm." Naturally Broch's attitude can't be explained solely along philosophical or intellectual lines. His skepticism was determined by the political and social circumstances of the dictatorship and the conditions of the Jews in Germany-Austria. "My next novel will be, without a doubt, a 'work of art.' I am sure that I will finish it during the imminent war. But I ask myself why, to what end, and for whom? Such thoughts reveal the profoundly immoral nature of my work."

Around 1936, Hermann Broch wrote: "Germany is a paranoid nation and it is disposed, as all paranoids, to rush out and confront nothingness, to fight for nothing with that mixture of fascination and anguish before death that has turned Germany into the greatest threat in Europe. Is it not significant that Heidegger, the philosopher of anguish and nothingness, should have become the most important of German philosophers?" At that time Broch was convinced that the Second World War was inevitable. He wrote in his letters of his premonition of "vast chemical warfare." On the occasion of Broch's fiftieth birthday, Elias Canetti made the following comment: "The work of Hermann Broch is situated between the last war and the present one. He may even be so sensitive as to detect chemical traces of the former in the air: and it seems that these lethal gases, which will surely exterminate us all sooner or later, have already begun to asphyxiate him."

The Death of Virgil

The Dutch transatlantic T.S.S. Statendam arrived in New York harbor on October 10, 1938, ten days after its departure from South Hampton. Hermann Broch stepped foot on land as if he had just been released from prison. He must have recalled his first visit to New York, in September of 1907, and the wonderment he felt upon witnessing the dynamic life of this great metropolis — the commerce, the factories and the promenades. He walked briskly, despite the weight of his suitcases. He was enveloped by the scent of the food, the imports, and the hazelnut trees surrounding the pier. He carried three hundred dollars in his wallet, and in his memory, the images of his mother and of Ea von Allesch. Shortly after his arrival he went to the National Bank of New York and opened an account in his name. At noon he visited the American Guild for German Cultural Freedom, a foundation that had awarded him a small stipend. Richard A. Bermann, its director, invited him to a meal. The employees of the foundation were charming people — kind, frank, straightforward, enthusiastic. He met Erich von Kahler at the luncheon, a Viennese professor in exile who would become his best friend in the United States. From their very first meeting Broch realized that von Kahler was exceptionally intelligent and kindhearted. In the afternoon he set off for his meeting with Albert Einstein at Princeton. They spoke two or three hours about the political situation in Germany. Broch thanked him for his letter of recommendation in support of his request for an American visa, and at nightfall he returned to New York. The next day he bought some adequate clothes for the winter season, he ate again with von Kahler, and he rented a room in a boarding house very close to Columbia University. The first six months were not terribly difficult.

Back in 1937 he had completed "The Return of Virgil," a short story written for the cultural program of a Viennese radio station, and he spent the following nine months developing a sequel to the story. He concluded "The Story of His Death," concerned with the final chapter of the poet's life, in Bad Aussee prison. When he left Vienna he carried three distinct versions of the text in his portfolio. Without realizing it, he was embarked on a project that would ultimately consume seven more years of his life. *The Death of Virgil*, a novel considered by many to be Broch's masterpiece, would describe the last eighteen hours of the Roman poet, from his arrival at the port of Brindisi until his death at Caesar Augustus' palace. Hermann Broch based this novel on a legend he had discovered in a copy of the *Aeneid* dating from the end of the seventeenth century, according to which Virgil had intended to destroy his epic poem. Although *The Death of Virgil* is written in third person, it is actually a monologue in which the poet addresses himself. Throughout its pages, prose and verse alternate to the point of confusion. Broch's interior monologue is quite different from Joyce's or Proust's or Thomas Mann's. The epic genre typically depended on the most unmusical of literary resources, that of discussion. Conversely, the lyrical genre had always rested on a musical foundation. If one considers Broch's five hundred and fifty-page novel as a lyrical exercise, one notes that it was composed according to the principles of a quartet, or more exactly, that of a symphony, as it is distributed in four parts — water, fire, earth and ether.

As much as *The Death of Virgil* is a novel about death, it also speaks about life. Virgil lived in an époque that shared many characteristics with Broch's. "A time full of blood, horror and death," to borrow Von Kahler's words. "A time of conquests, transformations, struggles and initiations." As Virgil takes up the personal challenge of writing the *Aeneid*, he finds that he is engaged in a parallel task of social critique and commentary. Yet he is obliged to compromise his personal viewpoints in reverence to the demands of the political establishment, and this conflict begins to affect his morale. He is plagued with doubts and uncertainties. Caesar Augustus, incapable of understanding the poet's turmoil, interjects:

"Listen to me,Virgil. I am your friend and I am also familiar with your work. The Aeneid is the most noble of all reservoirs of knowledge. All of Rome is captured in it — her gods, warriors and country dwellers alike — and I am astonished at your vast knowledge of our glories and pieties. In this composition you have made Roman space your own, as you made Roman times your own in previous works, and you rightly trace our lineage to our great ancestors, the Trojans.You captured everything perfectly [. . .] Isn't that enough for you?"

"Captured? [. . .] Quite right, captured [. . .] I wanted to capture everything, past and present [. . .] But I failed."

"How can you say that,Virgil?"

"My thirst for knowledge consumed me [. . .] I wanted to capture everything [. . .] This is what literature is for [. . .] It was my duty to capture the totality of our experience [. . .] I was impatient for knowledge [. . .] Such is the purpose of literature, and there is no other medium that can serve this function as well."

"I couldn't agree more,Virgil. At its best literature captures all of reality, and in that sense it is divine."

Caesar had failed to understand him. No one had understood the truth of the matter. No one cared to recognize the illusory nature of beauty.

Virgil wants to destroy the Aeneid because he rejects the notion that beauty should be at the service of the powerful, a source of gratuitous felicity. Possessing an acute sense of his own weaknesses, the cry of Aeneas becomes his own cry. Caesar Augustus and his friends do not understand his obsession with burning the work. On his deathbed Virgil returns to the same point: "Nothing on earth is divine. I sang to Rome, it is true, but my art has no more value than the statues in the Mecenas gardens. Rome shall not be redeemed by the grace of her artists. Her works of art shall be demolished, the Aeneid shall be burned."Virgil searches for himself unceasingly with adolescent disquietude. The thirst for knowledge as it relates to creative endeavors becomes the manifest theme in the most conventional part of the novel, the dialogue between Virgil and Caesar. The two men incarnate polar opposites, Art and the State. Virgil is reluctant to compare the *Aeneid* with the victories of the Roman armies, and he struggles to convince Caesar that his work is not state property. Moreover, the *Aeneid* is inconclusive. The culminating moment is lacking: the experience of his death.

The Death of Virgil represents an exploration and re-conquest of language, an act of faith in the power of literature. It is, moreover, a nearly untranslatable novel. The German language employs the noun, in a certain sense, as if it were a sentence or condensed phrase unto itself. Its capacity of constructing compound terms knows no bounds. In English, French and Spanish, the noun has a less elaborate syntactical function. Compound terms are rare. In accordance with the very structure of the German language, the strength of *The Death of Virgil* and its musical power lie with its nouns: their diverse permutations always hearken back to the central themes. Unfortunately, many of the translations on the market, in their efforts to approximate the idiosyncrasies of the original, leave the reader with a practically illegible text.

"The literature of Hermann Broch could be understood," wrote George Steiner, "in view of the totality of his ideas and works, as an incessant metaphor of translation: translation of the present time into the time of the final days, of classical values into contemporary chaos, or of verbal expression into music and mathematics." There is even a cinematographic quality to his literature: "Stirred by a contrary wind, metallic blue, nimble, malleable and faint, the waves of the Adriatic Ocean greeted the imperial squadron as it approached the port of Brindisi, gradually drawing closer, having left behind the hills of the Calabrian Coast." All the elements and forms of expression found in *The Death of Virgil* — the compound nouns, the monologues written at times in the form of a poem, the long and reiterative phrases, the musical rhythm and its counterpoints, the analysis of and reflection on language, the critical rupture from the traditional novel — make it one of the most complex and profound works of modern literature.

In the United States Hermann Broch dedicated himself to finishing *The Death of Virgil* and *Bewitchment*. In March of 1939 he fell into a profound state of depression. Thanks to a patron, Henry S. Canby, editor of The Saturday Review of Books, he was able to retire to the country and rest a few months. Spring in Killingworth, Connecticut reminded him of the landscapes in Austria. He realized then for the first time that his exile was irreversible. Memories of Vienna haunted his stay in the house of the Canby family, in consonance with the solitary silence enveloping the pines along the pathways. He was no longer the textile contractor who considered it necessary to renounce his paternal inheritance, nor the writer convinced that he should publish the "Resolution of the League of Nations." He was presently an Austrian exiled in New York City, a nearly unknown writer, a Jew obsessed with Virgil, a Viennese without a city whose memories grew ever paler.

In May of that year his circumstances grew even more complicated. The American Guild for German Cultural Freedom suspended its monthly delivery of one hundred and fifty dollars. Broch was left at the mercy of the elements, not knowing on whom he could depend for relief. Henry S. Canby came to his rescue once more. He granted him a residence of six weeks in the artists' colony of Yaddo, located in Saratoga Springs, near New York City. In this place Broch renewed his work on *Virgil*, and there he also met Jean Starr Untemayer, who would be the English translator of *The Death of Virgil*. The author and the translator worked six years together on the manuscript. From the start they considered publishing both versions of the novel simultaneously. They kept up a symbiotic relationship and the results were astounding. Her English version is an indispensable read for anyone who wishes to grasp the full meaning of the original. The two versions establish a congruency that clarifies and confirms their counterpoints. Jean Starr Untermayer was a translator with a magnificent ear, bursting with intuition and skill. In her English translation she substituted the present indicative for the preterit. She also trimmed some extremely lengthy phrases and searched for more precise verbs. Ultimately, her translation may be read as if it were an original.

When his six weeks in Yaddo were finished, Hermann Broch hadn't even two dollars for the laundry. Albert Einstein, who was always alert to his situation, invited him to live in his house at Princeton. Thornton Wilder made a habit of visiting Broch there on the weekends. They spoke of literature. They discussed *Finnegan's Wake* by Joyce, and they strolled about the city. In the evenings, Broch conversed with Einstein and read him parts of *The Death of Virgil*.

"Your *Virgil* is fascinating," Einstein assured him. "There is always a sense of mystery in it, something we sense but never quite understand."

The Struggle against Delirium

On September 1, 1939, Broch heard the news of the invasion of Poland over the radio. The German armies advanced on Warsaw. The signs
of the future were clear. The Second World War had begun. The months
that followed brought a sensation of stupor and anguish to Princeton.
Obsessed with the fate of his mother and Ea von Allesch, Broch was determined to acquire two visas for them, and in April of 1940 he bought
one in the Cuban embassy along with two passages on a transatlantic
ship. But Johanna Broch didn't want to emigrate; she insisted that at her
age leaving Austria would be the death of her. Her attitude revived some
old family grievances, provoking disputes over the inheritance, and the
inevitable childhood resentments surfaced once again.

Toward the end of 1941, Hermann Broch received a letter from
Thomas Mann: "The situation of your dear mother has moved me. I
hope that the danger is not imminent. I can imagine her anguish and
uneasiness. I assure you that you can count on me." Broch was always
conscious of the ambivalence he felt with respect to Thomas Mann.
Ever since the early twenties, he had been astounded by Mann's narrative power, and above all, the recognition and the success that he had
achieved as a writer. Thomas Mann was a writer of his very same era
and part of the world. All the characteristics of the German character
were present in his books. The mystery and the intelligence, the irony
and the gravity, the aspirations and the hopelessness, these were all undoubtedly German. But the Thomas Mann who wrote *Doctor Faustus* was
not the same one who had written *Magic Mountain*. His active militancy
against Hitler's barbarity gave way to the aloof intellectual of *Memoirs*

of an Apolitical Individual. Thomas Mann's protest against fascism was in some respects a protest against himself, that is, against his own political indifference during the First World War.

Mann assisted Hermann Broch in those difficult days, full of uncertainties. It was embarrassing for Broch to have to rely on Mann's prestige, to have to solicit time and time again his letters of recommendation. Yet the patriarch of German letters could open the doors of American foundations and universities for him. On October 30, 1940, he wrote to Broch: "A few hours ago I finished the letter of recommendation to the Guggenheim Foundation. My report is penned in a proud, strong and energetic tone. Of course, I included in it the lesson that you taught me regarding the novel [...] I cannot imagine a better theme for the patrons of the Guggenheim Foundation. I led them to believe that if they rejected my recommendation they shouldn't think of soliciting another from me ever again." Not surprisingly, the Guggenheim Foundation awarded Broch a fellowship for two years. Months later, Thomas Mann consigned in his diary: "We ate at home with Broch and von Kahler. Broch read us parts of his novel, *The Death of Virgil*. His story has gracefulness about it. It leads us to the very origin of Logos. There is a remarkable musicality to his text. After dinner we went to the library; there we spoke of our anxieties on the subject of evil. There is no exit nor refuge for the human spirit."

Hermann Broch wrote in a letter: "I want to dedicate the rest of my life to combating this plague known as fascism [...] I see grim times ahead. I see England and France under totalitarian regimes, and the United States under a National-Socialist dictatorship [...] Here there will be pogroms, organized according to the German model, that will seek to exterminate the Jewish race and which will end up killing all culture." He was convinced of the rise of Nazism in the United States. Racial discrimination was in vogue, capitalizing on the pride of white Americans. His essay "*Gone with the Wind* and American Slavery" (1941) expressed this fear. Broch felt that this movie posited the most radical declaration of White-American nationalism, the ideology of one's own land and one's own blood, of conquest and contempt. Many years later Joachim C. Fest, an historian of National-Socialism, revealed Hitler's admiration for *Gone with the Wind*. It was his favorite movie; he has seen it some twenty times.

At age fifty-six, Hermann Broch still exercised a strange attraction over women. In the United States, his Austrian charm was accentuated. He acted with simplicity and naturalness. He was clear and definitive in his intentions, without strain or bitterness, never allowing the emotions that governed him to affect his relationships with his closest associates. Hannah Arendt, who loved and admired Broch, referred to his gentility as *politesse du cœur*. In early 1941 Broch traveled to Cleveland and abandoned for a few months the women that were besieging him: novelist Fanny Colby Rogers, sculptress Irma Rothstein, his old friend Jadwigga Judd and Anne Marie Meier-Graefe, the widow of a renowned art historian who would later become his second wife. Hanna Arendt remembers that the apartment of Anne Marie in New York was like a Viennese household suspended in time. Unfortunately for Broch, the main impetus and enthusiasm of his life would remain behind him, back in Austria; exile would represent an irreparable loss to him.

One day in May, 1942, four agents of the Gestapo showed up at the apartment of Ea von Allesch in Vienna. They asked for Johanna Broch and the old lady received them as if she were waiting for them. She offered them something to drink and they conversed a while. Then, with the help of the servant, she descended the stairs and was ushered into the back of their truck. She searched for a seat and turned her eyes toward the house as the truck drove away. Without knowing it, she was bound for Theresienstadt, a death camp. Hermann Broch received notice of her death two years later. His son, Hermann Broch von Rotermann, managed to escape from Marsella to Portugal, and from there to New York. He married the daughter of novelist Jacob Wassermann and enlisted in the infantry of the U.S. Army. Each encounter with the Austrian refugees in America convinced Broch of the necessity of rescuing his friends and acquaintances that had remained trapped in Europe.

Beginning in June of 1939 he struggled to attain a visa and a stipend for Robert Musil. "The situation of Musil," he wrote to Ruth Norden, "is lamentable. Perhaps his gruff character warrants such conditions. Nevertheless, we should help him. Rudolf Olden initiated the negotiations in the Pen Club of London. We must write memos and recommendations and publish editorials in the newspapers. Musil is virtually unknown in England."

On November 9, 1939, Musil registered in his journal: "I have been informed that the Pen Club of London has abandoned the initiative of moving me to England. Olden sent me a copy of the signatures of support: Arnold Zweig, Hermann Broch, Rob Neuman, Thomas Mann. I was touched." When Broch discovered that he had failed in his negotiations, he wrote Musil a letter which was answered from Geneva: "It seems that I won't be able to leave Austria without a guarantee of financial support from the host country and under the assumption that I would be able to write productively there. I am afraid, however, that not even with all my dexterity will I be able to accommodate this requirement. I am pessimistic about my destiny, though I am convinced of the great future of culture in the United States." Broch was exasperated by his compatriot's unreasonable lack of confidence. However, not long thereafter Musil was imploring Broch's assistance: "Dear Broch: I gave Carl Selig the documentation you need [...] The moment has come to save the little, the very little I have left [...] For this, I am grateful to you for your help. Still, I am in doubt as to how I might survive in the United States. [...] You know that I am not capable of writing anything other than *The Man without Attributes* [...] How could I do otherwise? I am not expecting you to have an answer to this question." Unfortunately, news came soon that the Rockefeller Foundation had rejected Musil's application. Thomas Mann's petitions on Musil's behalf had been unsuccessful. Before Broch could think of another solution, Robert Musil had died in Geneva on April 15, 1942.

Hermann Broch spent that year rounding up friends and resources, attempting to convince various American foundations and universities that the exiled Austrian and German writers and intellectuals were of great importance to the future of the nation. After certain negotiations and explanations he attained a visa for the writer Franz Blei, who arrived in New York at the conclusion of the summer. But at age seventy, Blei was incapable of adapting and surviving outside his homeland. He died the following year in Westbury Hospital on Long Island. Broch had kept vigil by his side until his death. While Blei lay dying, Broch felt as though all of Austrian culture was languishing there with him. It was nighttime when he left the hospital. A slow drizzle began falling on the streets. Broch walked toward the train station. Franz Blei, he thought, represented the most eccentric voice in Austrian literature, and his work provided one of the most conclusive testimonies of Central European culture.

On the train back to Princeton he remembered Blei's intentionally ironic proposal — a law by which each citizen, upon turning fifty years old, should be required to write the story of his or her life, a balance of his or her hopes and failures. Yet very few grasped the irony of this proposal, for it was actually an impassioned defense against the totalitarian regime. One hundred years before Blei, Johann Gottlob Fichte, the great philosopher of German idealism, had imagined a perfect state in which the passport of every citizen, without exception, should contain his detailed biography. Such passports would threaten the creation of novels, since no detail of one's past would escape the control of the authorities. Blei's life, on the contrary, signified the rejection of the totalitarian state and the recuperation of the imagination, the healthy anarchy of literature. The literature of Franz Blei incarnated the secret dreams and the sense of humor and parody that defined that era of decadence.

Broch's Guggenheim fellowship expired before *The Death of Virgil* could be published. He envisioned a solution in the form of an old dream of his, lecturing at a university. Perhaps the New School for Social Research at Princeton might offer him a position as a professor. Unfortunately, his dream of a life in academia wouldn't be realized, since the New School didn't even have the funds to take him on as a

research assistant. Broch tried to get a new fellowship from the Rockefeller Foundation, this time in the area of social sciences and psychology. He presented a proposal of two hundred pages on the psychology
of the masses. The functionaries of the Rockefeller Foundation delayed
their approval of his solicitude. The recommendations of Albert Einstein, Thomas Mann, Erich von Kahler and professor Hadley Cantril
triggered the advancement of the fellowship, and starting in May of
1942, Hermann Broch received two thousand dollars annually, a sum
which, incidentally, hardly served to meet even his most rudimentary
expenses. "The more I study the psychology of the masses," he wrote,
"the more I realize that it is impossible to contain the subject. This project exceeds the capabilities of any single individual. It is necessary to
be well informed in psychology, history and sociology, and as if that
weren't enough, to master their respective grammars and methodolo-
gies. At sixty I was challenging myself to return to the impeccable logic
of mathematics, since I believed that I could achieve something in that
field. Now I find myself immersed in the psychology of the masses [...]
and although my investigations in this field are presenting great difficul-
ties for me, I feel that it is one of the few means by which a theoretician
may have a real impact on politics."

His "Theory of the Delirium of the Masses" (1948) was a sketch of
which he published fragments in various magazines. Broch's views on
the psychology of the masses, a theme that was fashionable in the decade
of the forties, distinguish themselves from that of other theoreticians —
such as Gustave Lebon, Sigmund Freud, Wilhem Reich, Ortega y Gasset
and Hadley Cantril — by one attribute only, their emphasis on the "conversion" of the masses to democracy. The third chapter is entitled "The
Struggle against Delirium," and it is a critique of fascism. Broch was
attempting to define a particular psychological mode that he called "a
crepuscular state" (Dämmerzustand), that is, a kind of mass trance that
he thought of as a measurable and concrete reality. However, it is in his
novel *Bewitchment* where this crepuscular state finds itself exemplarily
described, not in his academic studies on the psychology of the masses.
The story of the lynching of Mrs. Gisson gives us a precise idea of how

the sensibility of an entire community can be degraded to the point that its constituents surrender to hysteria and their hysteria transforms itself into violence. The five hundred pages of his studies on the delirium of the masses were, to a degree, the antechamber to an unrealized passion, the book of politics that he never wrote.

His essay "A Realization of Utopia" (1950) sharpened his ideas on politics even more. His concept of *absolute terrain* implicated the recognition of human rights as a moral imperative that should be integrated into everyday politics. If democracy were basically about voting on Election Day and counting the votes properly, as Churchill had remarked, then it would amount to little more than a vulgar competition between two or more political parties. For Hermann Broch, however, democracy was an indispensable tool for human rights. All utopian political systems have centered on the belief in one exclusive solution for the host of our social problems. Once this singular response is discovered, it is believed that all others ought to be rejected as erroneous. The Nazi and Soviet death camps, their absolute rein of terror, were due to this obsession for a single "true" response. For Hermann Broch, human rights were more than an ideal. He establishes in his essays that human relations are enabled by the concept of interdependence and that the moral imperative of universal brotherhood requires no proof or demonstration. "The unavoidable obligation" of lending assistance weighs on all of us, and this is the human right *par excellence*, the most fundamental human right.

The Order of the House

On the 22nd of April of 1942, The New York Times reported on the prizes of the American Academy of Arts and Letters. The winners in literature were Hermann Broch, Norman Corwin and Edgar Lee Masters. Broch was the first foreigner to receive this award. The thousand dollars served to pay his debts, above all those that he had acquired in his efforts to aid the Austrian refugees. In early July, Erich von Kahler proposed that Broch move in with him, since the first floor of his house was unoccupied. It was there that Broch found the security necessary to concentrate on reading and writing. It was as if the house located at Evelyn Place in Princeton were his very own. Kahler lived with his mother, Antoinette von Kahler, a lady of eighty years, intelligent and lucid, a specialist in English literature. Antoinette treated Hermann Broch as if he were her own son. For his part, he inspired an incredible force in her, stoking her uncommon passion for letters. They conversed every evening. He showed her the English translation of *The Death of Virgil*. They discussed the great epic poets and he assured her that their gift for storytelling had never been surpassed. She was a corpulent old woman with small eyes and thin hands, a prodigious conversationalist, possessing a vigor and imagination that astounded her son's friends. Broch lived in this atmosphere for six years (1942-1948). He put the final touches on *The Death of Virgil* in the house of von Kahler and in the company of Antoinette.

There are not many cases in literature — that of Samuel Beckett is an exception — in which the original and the translation were written virtually at the same time. *The Death of Virgil* is one such example. The final chapters were written in German and were translated into English with a difference of only a few days. Jean Starr Untermayer often grew frustrated because Broch was constantly making corrections to his work within hours of having written it. He also decided to modify parts of the first chapters and he would dictate all these changes to her over the telephone. The translator lived in New York and traveled to Princeton three or four times weekly. Unfortunately, the publishing house, Viking Press, rejected the manuscript at the last minute. Broch was informed that they didn't want or need another James Joyce. They feared that his book would be a bad investment. Afterwards, Kurt Wolff, owner of the publishing house Pantheon Books, picked up the novel and negotiated a loan with the foundation Independent Aid to publish it. Broch felt pressured by the editor. He refused to publish the novel because he wanted to write a fifth version. Four years earlier Thorton Wilder had written him: "The more I read *Finnegans Wake* the more I realize that Joyce worked too long on the book. By the time he completed it, it was too late; he had already missed the creative moment. I am saying this very much in earnest. Don't let the same happen to you with your *Virgil*."

The Death of Virgil was published at the end of June of 1945, in English and German simultaneously. A week later Marguerite Young wrote "A Poet's Last Hours on Earth," a long review in the *New York Times Book Review*. But bad luck embittered Broch's triumph. A strike of the linotypists paralyzed the newspaper and the Sunday edition in which it was to appear was never distributed. Despite this early obstacle, the following months brought an avalanche of commentaries on and reviews of the novel. Broch's relative anonymity was over. Ernst Bloch, exiled in New York, quipped: "You're lucky the Americans didn't demand that you present an endorsement from Virgil himself." And Thomas Mann wrote, years later: "I believe that *The Death of Virgil* is one of the most extraordinary and profound experiments that has ever been executed with the flexible form of the novel. When I said this in public I was faced with the patent opposition of many people, including certain individuals who supposedly possessed good literary judgment and taste. How could I, they said, praise this book: an obscure novel full of sophisms, an insufferable read? Nobody could convince me of changing my opinion. I will always recognize it as an extraordinary work."

But *The Death of Virgil* was a commercial failure. Pantheon Books was hardly able to pay off its loan to the foundation Independent Aid and Hermann Broch was paid next to nothing. The publishing house Routledge and Kegan of London delivered forty-five dollars for the rights, and Peusser Press of Argentina two hundred and fifty. Broch revised the French edition for more than two months, discussing confusing passages with Albert Kohn, the translator. But he didn't receive a franc. Gallimard released it a year after his death.

At the conclusion of the Second World War, Hermann Broch returned to a psychoanalyst's couch. Paul Federn, one of the most intelligent disciples of Freud in the United States, admitted him as a patient. The treatment was brief but intense. He was going to turn seventy. Those months he spent in therapy with Federn were dedicated to addressing matters of conscience: the horror and guilt he retained over the death of his mother and his immoderate preference for various women. He returned once again to the suffering of his infancy with all the mysteriousness and equivocations to be found in those formative experiences full of fear, quibbles, rites, taboos and suspicions. It meant a return to the most intimate memories of his childhood and youth, that infantile domain so closely related to the vegetable or animal world (as Jean Cocteau would have it), where all things turn about the murderous power of the father. He wrote to Ernst Pollak: "This is the first time in the history of my psychoanalytical treatment that I am quite certain I will be cured [...] Before, in Vienna, the possibility of a cure had only been hypothetical [...] Perhaps my confidence at present is due to the consummate skill of my analyst [...] If one day I send you news of my imminent marriage you will know that I have been cured." He sent Federn a fragment of his autobiography in 1943. The analyst replied that if Broch hoped for a successful therapeutic outcome he would have to rectify the partial quality of his self-analysis, for it appeared that he had amplified his relationship with his mother. Some four years later, Paul Federn, upon discovering he had cancer, committed suicide in his New York office.

When a man narrates his biography, regardless of the abundance of details and documentation in it (he may even choose to furnish medical bills and bar receipts), it will always be an imaginary reconstruction. Psychoanalysis concerns itself with the story behind the story, the latent content of the patient's story as it unfolds during the analytic hour.

Hermann Broch's fear of surrendering himself to a woman defined his last years. Anne Marie Meier-Graefe broke through his defenses. She was a woman who incited and provoked him in many ways. She was only a few years younger. Her admiration and respect for Broch and his work was the index of their solidarity and mature love. She didn't need to be conquered, adored or seduced. It could be said that he had never felt so protected and loved by any other woman before. He may have understood then that his previous relationships had been more about delight than love, more about deception than truth. But Anne Marie came a bit too late. At sixty, Broch's vitality was waning and his exile was extremely troublesome. He was tired of living from fellowship to fellowship, from alms to alms, and more importantly, he had lost his faith in literature. He had acquired American citizenship two years before, but not even as a citizen was he able to obtain his desired academic post.

Exceptional news from Europe came in the fall of 1945. Hermann Broch von Rotermann had marched into Vienna as an officer of the American Army of liberation. His letters, extensive and well written, were the window through which Broch contemplated a devastated Europe. Franziska von Rotermann, her hair graying, living in misery, had survived two bombardments and lost her family, but her will remained intact; she struggled on tenaciously. Ea von Allesch inhabited the ruins of her apartment, a shell without windows or doors. Twenty years before, her apartment, with its stylish English furniture, had perfectly complemented the elegance of its owner. When Broch's son found her, she was now an obese and stanch old lady dressed in rags and house slippers, huddled in a corner as she sheltered herself from the cold. At nightfall Ea would walk about with a velvet cloak over her shoulders among the ruins of Vienna, searching like many others for something to eat. As soon as he became aware of her condition, Hermann Broch wrote her every month, sending her comestibles and money. He never forgot what Ea von Allesch had done for his mother: the four years that she spent protecting her and the persecution to which she subjected herself for her sake.

As the postwar period began, Broch obtained a fellowship from the Bollingen Foundation to continue his research on the psychology of the masses. He aspired to convert his opinions into theories, to leave behind the ranks of essayists and to enter into the company of the philosophers. His essays on the psychology of the masses and on political questions were basically a reexamination of the past, a balance sheet of European culture over the past six decades. He made an effort at lending his work the form of a theory, a systematic body of ideas and knowledge, because, in his mind, literature — above all fiction — had lost its efficacy. In the tense climate of the postwar, as the true dimensions of the holocaust were being revealed, Broch saw that the task was even more daunting than he had imagined. Additionally, after the catastrophe of European civilization came the even more terrible threat of a conflagration be-tween the United States and the Soviet Union — the commencement of the Cold War. Hermann Broch was terrified by the possibility that his works and knowledge would be exploited by both sides and turned into merchandise, that they would only serve to reaffirm the immoral life against which he had intended to struggle. Something analogous hap-pened to the intellectuals of the so-called Frankfurt School. Theodor W. Adorno affirmed in those days that after the inferno of Auschwitz it was senseless to write poetry. Nonetheless, Broch never thought of Marxism as a theory of liberation. It seemed to him to be a secularized metaphor of Christianity.

The humanism of the young Marx, a theme that was fashionable in those days, had little to do with Stalin's *Realpolitik* in the wake of the meeting of the victors in Potsdam. "Russian imperialism," wrote Broch, "has become a war machine with no wish other than to initiate a world-wide revolution, a new world war." All his political essays of the period are concerned with the problem of democracy: "Theory of Democracy" (1939), "The Dictatorship of Humanism in a Total Democracy" (1939), "The City of Man: A Manifesto for Universal Democracy" (1940), "Strategic Imperialism" (1947), "The Division of the World" (1947), "Democracy in Times of Slavery" (1949), "A Utopia Realized" (1950), "The Intellectual in Conflict" (1950), "The Utopia of Human Rights and Responsibilities" (1950). Democracy was, for Hermann Broch, the insurrection of the individual against the totalitarian tendency that exists in any state machinery. He believed that the Marxist dream of a classless society and a society without a state had its origin in the same idea as democracy. But he wasn't convinced by the Marxist rhetoric of relations of production and value-labor. It all sounded like gibberish to his ears.

Broch had always refused to consider economics as the philosopher's stone of modernity. In the purest tradition of the Austrian School, the economy wasn't a question of convictions but a body of techniques. It could only be understood as a conjunction of technocratic measures. Our convictions, he was accustomed to saying, do not show us how to use the materials of construction in an engineering project. There was no fatalism in this conception of the economy, instead, a sense of opportunity: "The Marxists insist that anti-capitalist social measures can only be achieved through violent revolution, but how would they account for the example of England, where egalitarian reforms (whether one agrees with them or not) are the result of a democracy that permits democratic development in accordance with its unique national history?"

Hermann Broch focused his energies on discovering psychological laws rather than economic ones. He was concerned with the comportment of the individuals in certain critical situations. Karl Marx and Adam Smith, the mystics of the economy, chose to see in our emotions, passions, and loves, expressions of economic relations. But economic convictions, whether of the liberal or Marxist sort, can never be true convictions, because the only authentic convictions pertain to the field of morality. Despite the logical consistency of their theories, or perhaps because of this, they simplified reality in an inadmissible way and sur-rendered to fantastical perspectives that, without intending to, actually increased the unhappiness of humanity, relegating men and women to increasingly complex forms of slavery. The most persuasive discourse of modernity is, without a doubt, the discourse of science. Broch found this ironic since the masses are anything but "communities of scientists," and yet science had become the primary vehicle of persuasion and dom-ination. Not surprisingly, it happened that socialism wouldn't be fully serviceable until it became "scientific socialism," promising a paradise of happiness and liberty.

The persuasive power of modernity, anchored in the supremacy of science, had become something of a religion, as Broch saw it. But the scientist is not a prophet. "In the best of cases," says Broch, "he's a saint. The resurrection of the religious spirit in society requires an illumina-tion [...] Science cannot achieve such an illumination because it knows nothing of spiritual matters [...] It must content itself with paving the way for this illumination, instructing us on the material phenomena so that we may position ourselves better for the spiritual revelations to come." Hermann Broch's theories are equivalent to what Irving Howe has defined as the politics of uncertainty — a kind of politics that cannot save the world but without which the world would not be worth saving in the first place.

A Dilapidated Life

The year 1946 was plagued with doubts for Hermann Broch. He didn't know whether to return to Europe or remain in the United States. His friends were returning to Austria or Germany. They were unanimous in their hopes for the reconstruction of Europe. At times he wasn't eager to return. He hadn't forgiven himself for the death of his mother. He had failed, as he saw it, in a lamentable fashion. Erich von Kahler energized his daily life in those days, filling it with companionship and solidarity. In the evenings, when they conversed on the terrace, Broch spoke passionately:

"It doesn't bother me to be a man without a state. In this sense I am more Jewish than I ever imagined. I have identified all my life with the Diaspora. Though I know that misery is international, I don't presently want to face the misery in Austria. What I am concerned with, for the time being, is helping the survivors."

Erich von Kahler remembered Broch in this way: "Hermann was the ideal fraternal friend. But love of one's neighbor, when it is professed in earnest, precludes an intimate relationship. Agape kills Eros. This is why Alyosha Karamazov was incapable of loving anyone. There was a kind of transparency that characterized all Broch's relationships [...] One might spot him around town, armed with guides and train schedules, traversing enormous distances on the subway in order to arrive at his appointments and console his friends or request favors for them. One might also find him in his home after fifteen hours of work in front of his typewriter, keeping up with his correspondence in an extremely punctual fashion. Behind that tranquil façade, the pipe in his lips and his penetrating gaze, I sensed the tempests of internal anguish, alongside the felicity and consolation of his fraternal solidarity."

In March of 1947 Broch wrote to his son Hermann, who was working in Mexico as a translator at a UNESCO conference. He asked his son about conditions of life in that country. He was considering moving to Mexico City. During the war Anna Herzog had insisted on that possibility. She told him that the Mexicans were the nicest and most generous people on the face of the earth. Furthermore, Daniel Body, his editor, has been exiled in that capital city for a while. He himself, seven years before, in August of 1940, had tried to obtain visas from the Mexican government for some of his friends. He indicated to René Spitz, the psycholanalyst, that an official admittance into the country normally came with a price tag of nine thousand pesos. But Anna Herzog knew a certain lawyer named Becerra whose office was located at Ayuntamiento No. 14 and who would arrange the negotiations for only one thousand. His son responded to him that if he was thinking of emigrating it was unquestionably better to go to the south of France, where Anne Marie Meier-Graefe owned a house.

"Every day I receive dozens of letters but I don't have the money to pay a secretary. I am a very slow writer," Broch told Anne Marie, "and that is why I am a terrible polemicist. If I want to carry on with my true work I should limit my correspondence to that which is strictly necessary. These past few months I have aged with surprising rapidity and I realize with terror that I have wasted my life. My passion for writing letters has been my downfall."

The three volumes of his personal correspondence cover some thirty-eight years (1913-1951). In his letters one observes signs of creative audacity and the sober energy of an indefatigable writer. Lighting bolts of pessimism and personal hope crisscross his correspondence. His friends took great pride and pleasure in preserving his letters for so many years, as a memento of the inextinguishable spirit of his loyalty.

One particular morning, in a hurry and distracted, Broch came running to the home of Jean Starr Untermayer to pick up the translation of his text, "The Utopia of Human Rights." On his way out he tripped and rolled down the stairs. As he got up he felt a very sharp pain in his left leg. He couldn't walk and minutes later he fainted. An ambulance transported him to Princeton Hospital. He had fractured the neck of the femur and the doctors decided he should remain in the hospital. He spent ten months in bed. Luckily for him, all the charges were billed to the insurance of Jean Starr Untermayer. The period of the convalescence permitted him, among other things, not to have to worry about money. "The first weeks," he wrote Anne Marie Meier-Graefe, "were awful; lots of wasted time. But later, propped up in the wheel chair, I could write all day with no problem. I don't stop working at my typewriter until ten o'clock at night, when they turn out the lights." From that stay in the hospital came his essay, "Hugo von Hofmannsthal and His Time." It contains one of the most dolorous, analytical and lucid visions of the Austro-Hungarian Empire in decline. But more than that, it represents a return to his origins. In this manner he defended Austrian culture from the propagandistic historians whose apologetics, due to their glaring falsity, he found insulting.

The publishing house Bollingen was planning on publishing the works of Hofmannsthal in two volumes, and it contracted Hermann Broch for the prologue. In seven months he finished a long essay that constituted a review of Austrian culture and a critique of Viennese society. As he progressed with the prologue, he began to understand his own intentions with respect to the task. He wasn't interest in producing a literary critique or biography of Hofmannsthal. What he really wanted to accomplish would be more like a social assessment. The Empire always presented — both prior to and throughout its decline — the symptoms of the crisis that would envelop all of European culture. In Austria the crisis emerged with unusual intensity. In his novel *The Man without Qualities*, Robert Musil was obsessed with demonstrating that Kakania was the human incarnation of a modern world without foundations, without substance, or to put it another way, without a central value that would unite the different nations. These motives are perhaps most evident in his treatment of Ulrich's involvement with the so-called "Parallel Action." Musil may have perceived this absence of values as the cause of the nationalist strife and sense of unreality that characterized life during the decline of the Empire. The individual living in such a climate would have experienced a crisis of identity. His dreams would be deferred. He would have lost the capacity to order his life and govern his impulses. The Austrian writers who attempted to resist this crisis endowed their characters with an array of defense mechanisms. Their characters took refuge in obsessive regulatory rituals. Such is the meaning of the military uniforms of Joseph Roth, the Wall of China of Karl Kraus, and the disassociated intellectualism of Peter Kien in Elias Canetti's *Auto-da-Fé* — a character in retreat from reality, which he perceives as threatening to devour his dreams.

A Museum without Doors

Hugo von Hofmannsthal (1874-1929) was one of the finest writers of the *Finis Austriae* generation. He took up his pen at the twilight of the Hapsburg dynasty. Hofmannsthal understood that life in the Austria-Hungary of those days was little more than a question of survival, and in order to survive it was necessary to postpone any definitive decisions. Under these circumstances there was a temptation to flee from the real world. Fear of death became increasingly distressing in proportion to the progressive loss of faith in Austria-Hungary. Hofmannsthal detected a sense of desperation in the manners of his compatriots. The Empire that should have existed until the end of time had come crumbling down, and from its ashes emerged one of the bloodiest chapters in European history — not the Europe dreamed of by agents of democracy. The death of Franz Joseph marked the beginning of the end of a culture. Such was the crisis that was responsible for the deracinated Austrian psyche portrayed in the literature of the period.

In "Hofmannsthal and His Times," Hermann Broch proposed 1880 as the initiation of the euphoric catastrophes that ultimately destroyed the Austro-Hungarian Empire. From that point on, he affirmed, Vienna emerged as the most morally barren of European cities. "The spirit of an historical period is generally embodied in its architectural features. The architecture of the second half of the nineteenth century, the period in which Hofmannsthal was born, was without a doubt one of the poorest and saddest in European history. It was the period of eclecticism: the false baroque, the false renaissance and the false gothic. The styles of this period paid shameless homage to bourgeois dominion and solemnity, to a rigidity that evoked as much suffocation as security. If ever there were an attempt to cover up a moral abyss with rich trappings, it was then."

Despite his sharply critical tone, Broch refrained from executing a sweeping critique of art and society in the times of Hofmannsthal because he was primarily interested in the fate of the bourgeoisie, his own social class. The artistic currents he took into consideration were the operas of Wagner, the poetry of Baudelaire and impressionist painting, especially that of Cézanne. The profound insecurity of the bourgeoisie was a consequence of its ill-achieved political emancipation, reflected in the eclecticism of its architecture. The bourgeois man of the nineteenth century, condemned to political immaturity, compensated for this disadvantage with a romantic outlook that presumed to explain and make sense of reality. Nineteenth-century architects took special care with their façades, transforming Vienna and Budapest into precious filigrees of scenography, feeding the public's insatiable appetite for ornamentation. While most artists of the era were catering to the eclectic and romantic necessities of the bourgeoisie, noted Broch, in France Baudelaire and Cézanne had consummated a critical rupture with European poetic and pictorial traditions.

Hermann Broch analyzed the economic situation of the Austro-Hungarian Empire from the perspective of the bourgeoisie. The Hapsburgs and the aristocracy are only viewed in relationship to this class: "The unrealized dream of the Jesuit Counterreformation demanding a depoliticized, unitary life, ingenuous and simple, had inspired this Hapsburgs' politics for centuries. This was the legacy that Metternich had wished to preserve but his goals were never achieved [...] except, transitorily, in Vienna, for it was too late. From the archduke to the popular poet, the bourgeois man to the industrial proletarian, everyone seemed to share in the hedonistic attitude characteristic of the prevailing democratic style. In this sense, one could speak of a point of union between the nobility and the people [...] in accordance with that easy familiarity which is so specifically Austrian. [...] The social structures, however, were far from being truly democratic in the political sense of the term.

In fact it was the political inefficacy of the crown that was responsible for the conditions of decadence. The social structures had lost their sureness and Austria had become a kind of pseudo-democracy in which counts adopted the manners of coachmen and coachmen the manners of counts. The Empire found itself in a permanent state of dissolution. If it lasted as long as it did, it was merely because the period's splendor had a mesmerizing effect."

Hofmannsthal's Vienna was a museum without doors. His entire biography is condensed in the title of the second chapter of Broch's essay, "The Construction of a Personality in the Midst of Emptiness." Von Hofmannsthal, Jewish by birth, sought to obtain the noble title of artist. His was compelled to surpass himself, to be reborn with a fresh identity. But Hofmannsthal himself was the first to recognize that he couldn't achieve this solely by way of intimacy with the aristocracy, since no one can rise to a new social class merely by cultivating friendships with his or her superiors. Even membership in the proletariat is contingent on having been born into it. After all, one's pertinence to a social class confirms one's rightful place within a given society. "He who seeks to liberate himself from the class into which he was born will be repudiated by it and will become the object of its derision. He will be scorned in the manner of the *Freimann*, the executioner. In German, to belong to a social class implies being chained to it, and all social classes instinctively oppose the liberation of their members." Hugo von Hofmannsthal was a guest, the eternal guest of the charitable nobility, never a genuine bourgeois and still less a proletarian. His literary prestige demanded privileges that the bourgeoisie was disinclined to give him, and his quest for survival as an artist led him to increasing isolation. Von Hofmannsthal distanced himself from conventional bourgeois theater with his play *Death and the Fool*, and like Wagner in the world of opera, he produced one work after another employing ornamental scenography to support the mythological rituals transpiring on stage. Broch thought his plays were indicative of turn-of-the-century Austrians who found themselves in the midst of a moral void. To his mind, the era in question could be qualified as possessing all the characteristics of operetta. The spectacle became all the more phantasmal in light of the fact that the Empire was teetering on the verge of extinction.

Broch argued that Vienna in those days had become the living embodiment of the concealment of misery by wealth. Aestheticism served to dissimulate the few ethical values that remained, and as it buried them, it condemned itself. According to Broch's theory of values, all aesthetic values that do not emerge from an ethical principle are converted precisely into their contrary, kitsch. Vienna had become the capital of empty values, the metropolis of kitsch.

When he left the hospital, in February of 1949, Hermann Broch found his energies greatly diminished. Extreme tiredness is evident in his letters: "I am sixty-three years old [...] and my life is that of a gypsy. I have no sense of security. My insurance is in jeopardy because of the accident [...] and if something were to happen to me in the next few months, I would be ruined." When he returned from France, Anne Marie Meier-Graefe told him about the house she had bought in Saint-Cyr-sur-Mer and she proposed they should get married right away. Her suggestion of marriage was impossible because Broch's divorce hadn't been finalized yet. They were married three months later and in secret. Hannah Arendt and her husband Heinrich Blücker attended as witnesses. Around that time, Broch received a fellowship from Saybrook College of New Haven, Connecticut. It hurt him to leave Erich von Kahler, his apartment in Princeton, the beneficent routine of those final years, but he could no longer climb the stairs. His age and the historical circumstances weighed upon him every bit as harshly as a debilitating illness. As Anne Marie put the final touches on her house in the South of France, Broch rented a room in a New Haven hotel. "I've stopped writing stories because there's no sense in it," he wrote to Friedrich Torberg. "Ever since Hitler came to power I have refrained from literature because I am convinced that for our generation there can be no cause as important as fighting the plague of fascism [...] Still, I must confess that I continue to be tempted to write fiction, to tell stories and imagine characters. The wind at dusk, the various tones of the sounds on the street, a conversation at dawn. I am compelled to register and consign it all in a notebook, to rescue it all from oblivion."

In New Haven he met Thomas Mann and Thornton Wilder for the first time. On the occasion of Mann's seventy-fifth birthday, Yale University organized a ceremony in his honor, paying homage to his life and work. *The Story of a Novel* had been published a year before, Mann's diary of the creation of *Doctor Faustus*. In October of 1949, Hermann Broch wrote Erich von Kahler: "I just read *The Story of a Novel* and the most bitter feelings of inferiority were awakened in me. The old man's colossal force is astonishing. How could he have managed to write a masterpiece about the creation of his latest masterpiece? With that said, however, I must confess that his diary irritates me. His style is intolerable: 'Notice that I am a simple and generous man!' Such a style speaks less of Thomas Mann than it does of the immorality of literature."

Presentiments of the Abyss

Willie Weismann, owner of a publishing house in Munich, proposed adding Hermann Broch to his list of authors. From the dawn of the postwar he had wanted to publish Broch's book on the psychology of the masses. Then he made an interesting offer to compile his poetry, but Broch never felt that his poems were worthwhile. Two years later, he offered to publish his stories from the decade of the twenties. This time Broch accepted without conditions. The book contained five stories: "Methodically Constructed," "A Slight Deception," "The Cloud that Passes By," "An Evening" and "The Return of Virgil." As he corrected the galleys, he warned of his desire to rewrite the stories. He decided to include his first composition ever, "Canto 1913," in the collection, and he wrote two new stories for it. He also fashioned a new novel, *The Guiltless* (1949), which references three distinct time periods.

"Nineteen Hundred and Thirteen. What is my reason for writing? To once again consider my youth."

The plot of *The Guiltless* allowed him to reflect on his life and his engagement with literature. In it he revived the Middle European atmosphere as it had been prior to World War I. If there is a stellar protagonist in the novel it is the servant, Zerline, one of the most intimate and unfortunate of Broch's characters. Zerline worked more than thirty years in the home of baroness Elvira F. An attractive and beautiful peasant, her character incarnated the pride of the female gender. But she harbored resentment toward the baroness as a result of their class differences, and she felt compelled to take revenge on her. She sustained an impassioned romance with Mr. Juna, Elvira's lover and the true father of Hildegard, Elvira's daughter. Zerline fell in love with Juna, but like the Angel of Death, she destroyed him.

It is surprising to discover in *The Guiltless* a novel of operatic qualities, one whose characters — their risks, adventures and enthusiasms — stand as enduring expressions of kitsch. In it we are introduced to characters that represent the crisis of values with beguiling authenticity. A year before setting out to write *The Guiltless*, Broch included in his essay on Hofmannsthal the following observation on the operatic quality of the era: "Wagner understood that he was living in a time whose natural form of expression was the opera. He noticed that the bourgeoisie required a new meeting place in their cities to substitute for the ancient cathedrals, and that they sought to elevate the opera to that position. All that velvety grandeur illuminated with gas lamps responded to their idea of what modern art should be." *The Guiltless* confirms the demise of Don Juan, whom we see represented in the character of Mr. Juna. In true operatic fashion, the novel represents the triumph of kitsch, while exposing the guilty conscience of the age of innocence.

"Nineteen Hundred and Twenty-Three. What is my reason for writing? To once again consider humanity's failures."

All the characters of *The Guiltless* are distinguished by their political indifference, and for Hermann Broch, such an attitude was equivalent to moral perversion. Political innocence was indicative of moral guiltiness. The culpable innocence of the Austrian and German petty bourgeoisie had made possible the rise of Hitler. Such is the case of Zachary, one of the novel's protagonists, who invokes to the spirit of the German race to justify his personal acrimony.

Broch commented on the moral hypocrisy of his age as follows: "Any person who permits such cruelties as the atrocities of the concentration camps and gas chambers, but feels profoundly wounded and offended at any reference whatsoever to matters of sexuality is surely a hypocritical, savage beast."

"Nineteen Hundred and Thirty-Three. What is my reason for writing? To once again consider the promised land that we lost, to address my presentiments of the deepest abyss."

"Why offer the generation of the age of innocence a mirror in the form of a novel? Was it to demonstrate that, in the context of the abstract terror and crime of Nazism, European cultural traditions had been rendered meaningless, and the traditional forms of narration were no longer adequate to the novel? Was it to demonstrate that naturalism, the dominant narrative style of the nineteenth century, with its realism and veracity, was no longer sufficient?"

The disenchantment with literature that Broch experienced toward the end of his life was the culmination of a truly unfortunate passion. The genre of the novel seemed no longer adaptable to what the author saw and heard. Broch believed that James Joyce had clarified these problems with "extraordinary authenticity," for he had demonstrated that the chaos in the universe could only be properly represented with a multiplicity of resources: "symbolic constructions, condensation of symbols, multidimensional pathways." But would the petty bourgeois — assuming that he actually read Joyce's novels — recognize himself in the mirror of *Ulysses*? Would he realize to whom Joyce was referring when he created Leopold Bloom? Ultimately, what is the value of a novel of this type, or any other type?

The German public responded enthusiastically to *The Weavers*, a theater play by Gerhart Hauptmann, and to the works of Bertolt Brecht, but their enthusiasm did not bring about their conversion to socialism. Catholicism did not gain adepts with the literature of Claudel, nor the Anglican Church with the poetry of T.S. Eliot. The author reveals his convictions but the profound emotions he awakens with them belong to the field of aesthetics. "Only he who was convinced beforehand allows himself to be persuaded by a theater play or a novel," wrote Broch. He incessantly questioned the value of literature but found no answer to satisfy him.

Are artists truly able to lend dignity to human life through their artworks, and do they occupy a privileged position in this respect? The principle of eternity that artists would oppose to fugacity and the instant — are they not deluding themselves, and if not, are they truly better equipped than others to accomplish this mission? Are writers justified in assuming that literature can rescue our heritage from oblivion by constituting a lively remembrance of times past? Does appreciating literature truly help us to cope with the fundamental problems of eternity and death?

Broch's confidence in the affirmative responses to these questions waned as he aged.

Kindness and Intelligence

Midway through the summer of 1950, Hermann Broch was making plans to travel to Europe. After struggling for more than a decade, he finally acquired a post as a professor of German literature at Yale University. Unfortunately, his body was not up to it. "I am an ill and exhausted old man who was young for a long time. I have forbidden myself travel to New York. It is a needless expense of energy. I am presently writing fourteen hours a day." The Pen Club of Austria presented his candidature to the Nobel Prize in 1950, but there was no response from the other associations. The stimulus of the trip to Europe infused new spirits in him. He was anticipating seeing Anne Marie Meier-Graefe in Saint-Cyr-sur-Mer, enjoying the house where he would pass his elder years, conversing in Vienna with Ea von Allesch and participating in the Congress for Cultural Freedom in West Berlin (to which Marvin Lasky had invited him).

André Gide, Arthur Koestler, Bertrand Russell, Julian Huxley, Benedetto Croce, Carlo Levi, Karl Jaspers and John Dewey would be present at the Congress. Broch wrote "Intellectuals and the Struggle for Human Rights" for the occasion. He made the following comment in that paper: "Thanks to their belief in utopia and confidence in human dignity, intellectuals have contributed to determining the course of all revolutions throughout history [...] However, when a revolution is superceded by 'power' and the 'state,' its principles have been perverted and betrayed [...] This is why intellectuals, rather than complaining of an 'unhappy conscience,' should become strategists of *Realpolitik*, in other words, they should struggle inch by inch for the attainment and preservation of human rights."

One day in March of 1951, Broch fainted over his typewriter. He awoke in the St. Raphael Hospital of New Haven. According to the cardiologist he had suffered a heart attack resulting in myocardial damage. He was ordered strict repose, but Broch hadn't enough money to remain in the hospital, so he went home, promising to take care of himself. During his final weeks, he visited New York in the mornings. In his forever-inconclusive biography, he wrote: "I am slowly, implacably killing myself. I have killed myself working [...] I am killing myself over the very same conflicts that have defined my life. I have renounced all happiness and intimacy, and might renounce even my work and life itself, so as not to have to face these conflicts." He worked ten hours daily on *Bewitchment* during the final week of his life. It was a novel that he had been rewriting for over fifteen years. At six in the morning, on April 30, Broch died of a massive heart attack. The milkman found his body fallen over the suitcase full of clothes and books that he had thought to take to Europe with him for the conference. The participants of that conference were never to see him.

In *The Book of Elders* (a version of the Talmud dating to about 1,000 AD) there is a story which Hermann Broch liked very much and which nicely sums up his life: "A stranger came to visit a rabbi and asked him, 'Which is more important, intelligence or kindness?' The rabbi answered, 'Intelligence, of course, for it is the foundation of our humanity. But if a man has only intelligence and not kindness, it is as if he possessed the key to the master bedroom but had lost the key to the door of his house.'"

About the Author

José María Pérez Gay was born in Mexico City in 1943. He lived in Germany for fifteen years, where he took his doctorate in German Studies. He has translated – from German to Spanish – Goethe, Kafka, Thomas Mann, Hermann Broch, Karl Kraus, Robert Musil, Elias Canetti and Paul Celan. The German government awarded him the Grand Cross of Merit in 1992 and the Goethe Medal in 1995. The Republic of Austria awarded him the Austrian Cross for Arts and Sciences, First Class, in 1997. He served as Mexico's ambassador to Portugal under President Vicente Fox, and he has written several novels.

About the Translator

Eduardo Jiménez Mayo was born in Boston in 1976 and raised in San Antonio, Texas. He graduated with honors from Harvard University in 1999, with a Bachelor of Arts in Spanish Studies, and in 2004 he received his doctorate with honors in the same field from Madrid's *Universidad San Pablo-CEU*. In 2005, he wrote and published a scholarly book on the Spanish poet Antonio Machado (*El evangelio según Juan de Mairena*, Madrid: Editoriales Verbum), and he currently teaches literature at The University of Texas at San Antonio.

Printed in the United States
202672BV00002B/211-315/P